Making 'Imbeciles' of the Poor

*The Lives of People in the
Berwick-upon-Tweed Union Workhouse
categorised as 'Imbeciles'*

George C. Murray & Karen McKenzie

GCM RECORDS LLP

First published 2020
By
GCM RECORDS LLP
Berwick Workspace
90 Marygate
Berwick upon Tweed
TD15 1BN
enquiries@gcmrecords.co.uk

Copyright © 2020 Murray & McKenzie

All rights reserved. No part of the publication may be reproduced or transmitted in any form or by any means, electronic or mechanical, now known or hereafter invented, including photocopy, recording or any information storage or retrieval system, without permission in writing from the publisher.

Printed in the United Kingdom by Printspot (www.print-spot.co.uk)

978-1-913145-06-4

Cover image: *'Unborn Child at Berwick Workhouse'* by Paul Scotland

~ Acknowlegements ~

We are grateful to Linda Bankier, Berwick-upon-Tweed Archivist, and Friends of Berwick and District Museum and Archives, and staff at Northumberland Archives for their valuable guidance during the process of researching this book.

~ Contents ~

Foreword 7

Poor Law: 'Idiots,' 'Imbeciles,' and 'Lunatics' 11

Making 'Imbeciles' of the Poor 43
    Charting the Lives of People categorised as 'Imbeciles'
    in the Berwick-upon-Tweed Union Workhouse

From Poor Law to Medicine to Deinstitutionalisation 121
    Lessons Learned?

Afterword 133

References 136

Appendix 140
    Berwick-upon-Tweed Union Workhouse Timeline

~ Foreword ~

This book tells the stories of a group of 32 people living as Inmates of the Berwick-upon-Tweed Union Workhouse at the time of the 1881 Census, who were categorised as 'Imbeciles.' Thirty were adults and two were children. The youngest Inmates were a twelve-year-old boy, who was already classified as an 'Imbecile' on entry to the Workhouse, and a five-month-old girl, born to a woman categorised as an 'Imbecile' in the Workhouse and later categorised as an 'Imbecile' herself.

The book uses available records to chart these people's lives both before and after entering the Workhouse and how they lived prior to, and after, being labelled as 'Imbeciles.' The book looks at what function categorising people as 'Imbeciles' might have served in this era and the implications for the people concerned.

While the term 'Imbecile' is today used simply as a term of abuse, in the 1800s it was used as a way of categorising people who lacked the capacity to act independently. It was a way of identifying people who had neither resources nor the means of acquiring resources to look after themselves. An 'Imbecile' was also a way of classifying people with difficulties less severe than people who would be categorised as 'Idiots.' The latter were defined as people who were usually more severely disabled, with problems being evident since birth. An 'Imbecile' would be broadly equivalent to what would today be considered to be a mild or moderate intellectual disability. An 'Idiot' would be similar to what is now thought of as being a severe or profound intellectual disability.

The term 'Imbecile' comes from the Latin *Imbecillus*, meaning weak-minded. The term 'Idiot' comes from the Greek to mean a private citizen (as opposed to an official). The definition of 'Idiot' was subsequently extended to mean unskilled, ignorant, uneducated and common and, in the fourteenth century, to mean mentally deficient. Both 'Imbecile' and 'Idiot' were later adopted as diagnostic terms, until they were replaced by new terms that essentially meant the same thing but were considered to be less offensive.

'Imbeciles' and 'Idiots' were seen as distinct from 'Lunatics.' 'Lunacy,' from the Latin *Lunaticus*, refers to epilepsy and madness and relates to a belief in a connection between the moon and madness. The modern-day equivalent of a 'Lunatic' would be someone with a mental illness. Epilepsy, since the development of appropriate treatments, is no longer normally considered a mental illness, but is now thought to be a physical illness (a neurological condition). In the 1800s there were no effective treatments for epilepsy, so it was still considered a form of madness.

Today the term *intellectual disability*, which can also be referred to as *learning disability* in the United Kingdom, is used instead of 'Imbecile' or 'Idiot.' Intellectual disability is a term applied to people who have lifelong significant impairments in their intellectual and adaptive functioning, with an onset in childhood (American Psychiatric Association [APA], 2013). One difference between the term 'Imbecile' and more modern classifications was that 'Imbecility' could be acquired at any stage in life, so no distinction was made with people who had decline in their cognitive abilities in adulthood caused by illness, accidents or dementia. In the 1800s, 'Idiocy' was seen as having been present from birth, however, as we shall see, terms were not always applied consistently.

When reading this book, it is important to understand the context in which the language used in the classification systems of the 1800s occurred. It is, however, also important to notice how the terms, which originally were used to categorise people in need of support and protection, could subsequently acquire negative connotations when the systems designed to provide care failed to do so adequately.

The year 1881 was chosen as a starting point for a number of reasons. The Poor Law, which was an important contextual factor, had been well established at this time. It had gone through a number of revisions according to changes in government policies, often reflecting how it was used to control the population and its needs. Correspondingly, workhouses were embedded as a part of providing poor relief, but they had also evolved according to the policies and local arrangements reflecting their use. The year 1881 was also the last Census year before the 1886 Idiots Act, which heralded the beginning of establishing separate facilities for the care, education and training of '*Idiots*' and '*Imbeciles*.' The Lunacy Act of 1845 had already provided the policy context for people with a mental illness, resulting in the construction of a system of County Lunatic Asylums. In the absence of specific provision for people with an intellectual disability prior to 1886, people categorised as '*Imbeciles*' found themselves caught up in either the workhouse or County Lunatic Asylum systems if their needs could not be met by their families.

This book is based on information from the records that were kept at the time. The main sources of information about the people in this book were Census Records, Board of Guardians Minute Books, and Case Books from the Northumberland County Lunatic Asylum, as well as other historical documents relating to the topic. These records were often hand-written documents and establishing the accuracy of information was not always easy. Frequently, there were issues of handwriting that was difficult to decipher, inconsistent spelling, abbreviations that were not always defined, and a reliance on information being reported by people with varied levels of education.

There were naturally some gaps in records and some people's lives were easier to trace and describe than others. The available information has been verified and cross-checked whenever possible, however, there is some degree of speculation and interpretation in places.

The main aims of this book are: to acknowledge, chart, and provide a historical context for the lives of the people who were frequently perceived as being a burden to society; and to consider some of the lessons that can be learned from their lives in relation to how people with an intellectual disability are viewed and treated today.

Poor Law:
'Idiots,' 'Imbeciles,' and 'Lunatics'

People with an intellectual disability have often been represented as a sub-set of people referred to as *The Poor*. Poor people are often defined by their lack of independent means and people with an intellectual disability are defined by their lack of a means to be independent. Consequently, when the two are combined, life can be doubly impoverished. Various attempts have been made across the centuries to address this issue. Where there are the resources and capabilities for families to look after themselves, government intervention, at whatever level, has little role to play. When families lack resources, government intervention becomes necessary.

Defining and categorising people has primarily occurred for economic reasons and was less prevalent in pre-industrial societies. In those days, defining people as intellectually disabled was less necessary because, whatever someone's level of ability, there was generally something that people could do to contribute to the functioning of the community. The only exceptions would be those with more profound disabilities, with additional health conditions, for whom survival would have been difficult.

The advent of defining people by what they *could not* do occurs because the roles and tasks that allowed people to contribute to society changed or, with increased mechanisation, were no longer needed. This meant that those people were then seen as more of a burden or cost. Although such changes have occurred throughout history and still continue today, perhaps the most significant events occurred in the 1800s.

The Poor Law
The Poor Law Act of 1388 was introduced with the goal of addressing issues of labour shortages following the Black Death. Poor relief

attempted to alleviate the effects of poverty and historically it has been the responsibility of government and religious organisations. The Poor Law allowed for the provision of the basic necessary items for everyday living, for example, food, clothes, and shelter. The Poor Law was designed to provide assistance at times of emergency, for example, when there were bad harvests or if there was an economic downturn.

Two issues dominate the history of providing relief to the poor: who deserves relief and how should it be funded? Inevitably there have been long-standing difficulties in balancing meeting the needs of the vulnerable in society whilst trying to minimise the costs of those deemed to be capable of contributing but choosing not to.

The Vagabonds and Beggars Act of 1494 introduced punishment as a strategy. People considered to be vagabonds and beggars were punished by being put in the stocks, fed a limited diet, and later returned to the area where they came from. No police forces existed at this time and punishments were administered by volunteers from the local community. The Act, however, did not make any clear distinctions between vagabonds and the 'impotent poor' – the latter including the sick, the elderly, and the disabled.

In the 1500s, the effects of poverty increased as the population expanded rapidly, quickly outgrowing what the economy of the time was able to provide. In 1531, the Vagabonds and Beggars Act was revised. New provisions were made available for different categories of poor people allowing the sick, elderly, and disabled to be issued with licences allowing them to beg. The Dissolution of the Monasteries (1536-41) also led to a transfer of resources from the church to the crown, making care of the poor more difficult. The church had previously played an important role in supporting more vulnerable members of society.

The Poor Act of 1552 focused on using Parish resources as a fund to combat poverty. Two Overseers were appointed from each Parish to collect money and distribute it to the poor. This established the principle of providing for the poor as being the responsibility of the Parish, however, voluntary donations proved difficult to collect.

In 1563, Parliament passed new legislation allowing parishioners to be brought before a judge if they were deemed to have not been paying adequate funds to the Parish. Non-payers could be imprisoned until a contribution was made. In 1576, Houses of Correction were established, where able-bodied, non-working, paupers were put to work with the labour being the method of correction. The Act of 1578 then transferred the power to administer the Poor Law from Justices of the Peace to Church Officials in the area.

Towards the end of the 1500s, public authorities started to develop a more selective approach to the support of the poor. Clearer distinctions were made between the legitimately needy – the *deserving poor*, who were deemed worthy of relief – and the *idle*, who were not. The *deserving poor* were seen as those who were incapable of looking after themselves, for example, young orphans, the elderly and the disabled. The *idle* were people who were deemed capable, but too lazy to work.

The Poor Law of 1601 established Parishes as being responsible for their local communities. This Act made clear distinctions for Overseers of poor relief between:

The *Impotent Poor* – these were people categorised as being unable to work as a consequence of being elderly, blind, crippled or otherwise physically infirm. These people were usually cared for in a Poorhouse;
The *Able-bodied Poor* – these people were set to work in a House of Industry where materials were provided for them to work;
The *Idle Poor and Vagrants* – these people were either sent to a House of Correction or imprisoned;
Pauper Children – these would be found apprenticeships.

The 1662 Settlement Act allowed Parishes to work out who was entitled to relief in their area. This Act was aimed at deterring people from moving to more generous Parishes. It was made clear that Parishes were only responsible for the people who belonged to them. People needed to demonstrate a significant connection to the Parish before they were entitled to relief, for example, they needed to have been born in the Parish, have a connection by marriage, or have worked there for a period of time. Overseers were given powers to move people on who were not considered to belong to the Parish.

There were some practical problems with the Settlement Act. It was not always easy to define who belonged to the Parish. There were also practical difficulties in making arrangements for poor people to go back to their originating Parish. Sometimes Parishes were required to make arrangements for reciprocal payment systems with other Parishes.

The Vagabonds Act of 1752 established a more structured system of collecting resources for the Parish, effectively turning donations into a form of taxation. The Parish would determine the level of funds required to provide for the poor and Justices of the Peace would grant the authority to determine the amount of donations by the Parish's wealthier property owners. Clearer distinctions were made between categories of vagabonds, and levels of punishment for vagabonds deemed to be able-bodied were increased, including the introduction of hanging for persistent begging.

Thus, during this period there were a number of important developments. The Poor Laws required each Parish to appoint an Overseer of the poor. The Parish was made responsible for implementing public charity and it was required to levy a Parish tax, known as the Poor Rates. This was largely levied on people with significant property. Parishes were also given the powers to require the poor to work, to set up apprenticeships for children, and to maintain those unable to work through incapacity.

The early Poor Laws had some clear advantages. As the system was administered locally, it was known who in the Parish was in need of help. Assistance could, therefore, be tailored according to individual, family, or local needs. They also, however, had some significant disadvantages. The Poor Laws led to practices that were stigmatising. People could be punished for not working and be placed in a House of Correction. Parishes could also make distinctions between who was *deserving* and *undeserving* of support, with the result that those defined as *undeserving* could be denied relief or made to work for it. No specific rules existed about how to distinguish the *deserving* and *undeserving*; it was up to each Parish to decide how this was done.

Workhouses and The New Poor Law

In 1723, the Workhouse Test was introduced. This established the principle that, if a person wanted to receive poor relief, they had to enter a workhouse and undertake a set amount of work. This test was designed to deter people from making irresponsible claims on the Parish resources. The 1782 Act created opportunities for Parishes to combine to provide poor relief across county areas. Parishes became organised such that they could set up workhouses between them, allowing a more efficient use of pooled resources. These workhouses were intended to only provide for the orphaned, the sick, and the elderly, and not the able-bodied poor. The plan was that the able-bodied poor would receive relief in their own homes.

Two key factors – the effects of the Industrial Revolution and the end of the Napoleonic Wars – led to the revision of the Poor Laws and changes in the way in which support was provided. These factors were also influential in shaping the way in which intellectual disability was defined – in terms of *inability*, rather than *ability*. The first of these factors, the Industrial Revolution, not only mechanised the production of goods, but it also transformed farming. Tasks that had previously been carried out by people were taken over by machines. This not only replaced the need for the role of people in the production of goods, but it also created the need for a more highly skilled and educated workforce. The end of the Napoleonic Wars in 1815 reduced the need for large numbers of young men to go into the army. Warfare up until this point largely had comprised the relatively unsophisticated and unmechanised process of large numbers of opposing groups of men engaging in face to face conflict.

By the end of the 1700s, the costs of providing relief were increasing as inflation caused by the Napoleonic Wars sent more people into poverty. By the beginning of the 1800s, it was estimated that 10-15% of people were in receipt of poor relief. As a result, the system of Poor Laws in place became economically unsustainable and a New Poor Law was introduced in 1834, with a new emphasis being placed on the role of workhouses.

The 1834 Act was underpinned by a belief that the Poor Laws encouraged poor people to be indolent by giving them relief. There was concern that local Parishes were too generous and that poor people had a growing expectation of welfare, which discouraged them from feeling the need to work. Large groups of able-bodied people were assumed to be capable of working. One main difficulty with this line of thinking was that work was not always available in some areas or the work available was paid at levels less than subsistence.

The 1834 Act contained some key principles. Embodied in the Act was the belief in the need to be punitive. This was aimed at making the receipt of relief less favourable than working. The Workhouse Test was one of the ways in which this was achieved, by making life worse than if the poor were supporting themselves independently. There were, however, some practical constraints on how this could be done. It was recognised that it was unwise to give people less money, as often they were already living below subsistence level. Further exacerbating public health issues such as malnutrition would not help improve the conditions of the workforce. As a result, the delivery of poor relief was made contingent on people going into the workhouse. This would mean fewer people would receive outdoor relief and it was intended that a series of new workhouses would be built to meet this need.

On entering the workhouse, the poor would receive food, clothing, and bedding, however, in order to make it unpleasant, practices were introduced such as splitting up family groups, and requiring Inmates to wear uniforms and carry out hard labour. It was intended to make life dehumanising and harsh, with the idea that this would deter people from seeking relief and save money as a consequence.

The 1834 Act also embodied the principle of the centralisation of services. It attempted to take some decision-making power out of the hands of local Parishes, by requiring them to join together in a collective to pool resources. Parishes were also expected to set up new workhouses. Central oversight was by Poor Law Commissioners, who were based in Somerset House. There was a small number of Commissioners overseeing many unions, within set districts. Attempts were made to standardise the delivery of poor relief across the country, with the aim of moving away from local, face to face delivery of poor relief. A uniform system of tax was introduced across all union areas. The Irremovable Poor Act 1846 (updated in 1861), established the principle that the Union Board of Guardians was responsible for the delivery of poor relief to people who had been resident in their area for three years.

These new ways, however, were not always adhered to. Many Parishes acted to frustrate the actions of Commissioners and the principles of relief being provided through workhouses. At a practical level, it was expensive to build the larger workhouses which were needed to house entire families, therefore, in many areas Parishes continued to provide the majority of relief in people's homes. There were also problems with the ideology of workhouses being used for putting the able-bodied to work and many were not always used for this purpose in practice. In many areas, workhouses were not primarily used for the indolent poor, but rather as places for the care of people who were sick, elderly, orphaned, mentally ill, and disabled.

The New Poor Law did, however, begin the formalisation of medical health care to people. The Act required Medical Officers to be appointed who would assume the responsibility for local districts and infirmary wards in workhouses. In 1842, the General Medical Order set out standards of practice for Medical Officers and these are often seen as the forerunners of the principles that would be later enshrined in the National Health Service.

The 1834 Act makes a distinction between *Indoor* and *Outdoor* relief, with the aim of phasing out *Outdoor* relief and forcing paupers into receiving *Indoor* relief in order to encourage them to look after themselves. The workhouse was designed to be intentionally harsh with hard labour. Only the most poor and destitute were meant to access such a resource. Some attempts were made to run workhouses at a profit and work could consist of tasks such as breaking stones or breaking bones to make fertiliser.

As with many Government policies today, which attempt to address the unplanned consequences of previous poorly considered policies, the new workhouse policy was not without its problems. The Poor Law may have become expensive, but the new policy of institutionalisation was not going to be without its costs. Berwick-upon-Tweed, with its unique position in relation to the rest of England, was able, to some extent, to influence how the new policy was implemented in the local area.

Berwick-upon-Tweed

Berwick-upon-Tweed held the unusual position of not being a part of any county but was, instead constituted as being a '*County of a town corporate.*' At the time, this placed it in a similar position to the Isle of Man and the Channel Islands in that, although it was a dependency of the Crown of England, it retained significant powers of self-governance. It was independently governed by a Guild of Freemen up until the 1835 Municipal Reform Act. Berwick-upon-Tweed had its own Sheriff, court and jail. Since the reign of Philip and Mary in the 1500s, the town of Berwick-upon-Tweed had returned two members to the English House of Commons, elected by the Burgesses of the town.

As far back as the 1100s, during the reign of Alexander I, when Berwick-upon-Tweed was a part of Scotland, it was capital of the district called Lothian. Over time, Berwick-upon-Tweed grew into a wealthy town and became the chief seaport in Scotland. It had a castle, churches, hospitals, and monastic buildings.

Throughout the 1800s, the town had many areas of manufacturing including sacking, sail cloth, cotton, and muslin. It produced woollens, such as stockings, carpets, felts, and hats. Leather manufacturing took place with tanneries producing leather for saddlers and glove, boot, and shoemakers. Other manufacturing took place with production of ropes, nets, nails, snuff, tiles, and bricks, as well as coach-making, brewing, fish processing, and printing.

Shipping took place between Berwick-upon-Tweed and Leith (now part of Edinburgh), Glasgow and London, with trade in wool, potatoes, eggs, butter, candles, pork, barley, wheat, flour, corn, herring, paper, leather, tallow, canvas, and sacking. Trade further afield occurred between Berwick-upon-Tweed and Norway, Sweden, Russia, Prussia, Holland, and Denmark, with exchanges of timber, iron, hemp, flax, tallow, tar, wheat, barley, and oats.

The area also had a number of fisheries supplying local markets with salmon, lobsters, crab, herring, cod, ling, turbot, skate, and flounders. Local butchers' markets offered beef, mutton, veal, lamb, and pork, while poultry markets sold goose, turkey, duck, pigeon, and chicken. Green markets sold a range of local produce, including cabbage, potatoes, onions, leeks, peas, beans, carrots, turnips, radishes, artichokes, celery, lettuce, and cucumbers. There were also markets for corn, eggs, and butter, as well as woollens and cloth.

In Tweedmouth, which was south of the river, there were also a number of industries, including foundries, boat slips, a herring boat depot, boatbuilders, coal yards, timber yards, a sawmill, a pipe manufactory, smithies, tanneries, a boiler yard, and a dairy. In Spittal, at the mouth of the Tweed, there was a bone mill, a gas works, a lifeboat station, an iron works, and a quarry, as well as a well-established fishing community. Slightly further afield, Scremerston offered a lime works, while collieries existed at Deputy Row, Unthank, Bowsden, and Etal. In the country areas surrounding Berwick-upon-Tweed, the main occupations were in farming, including the required support services, such as blacksmiths and millers.

Conditions for the Poor in Berwick-upon-Tweed

Despite Berwick-upon-Tweed being a thriving town in the 1800s, a section of the population experienced extreme poverty and squalid conditions. In his *'Report to the General Board of Health on a Preliminary Inquiry into the Sewerage, Drainage, and Supply of Water, and the Sanitation Condition of the Inhabitants, of the Parish of Berwick-upon-Tweed, in the County of the Borough and Town of the same, including the Townships of Tweedmouth and Spittal'* (1850), in relation to the Public Health Act, Robert Rawlinson, Esq., Civil Engineer, Superintending Inspector, described condition in the poorer areas of Berwick-upon-Tweed at that time:

> *'The principle part of the expenditure of this Parish is caused by paupers who reside in damp and badly ventilated houses in Wallace's-green, Walkergate-lane and Chapel-street.'* (p17)

He further goes on to describe problems where owners of slum properties and/or their agents often lived in the same neighbourhood as the paupers. Poor relief officers paying the relief to paupers were frequently:

> *'watched by such persons, and, after he had paid the relief as directed, the landlord or his agent would immediately claim it for rent. So it may be fairly assumed that the Parish pay to the support of the very places which tend to create paupers and increase the rates.'* (p18)

Robert Rawlinson subsequently describes the condition of housing in these areas of town: *'the street is wide and open, but unpaved; the ramparts, however, block ventilation, and make those houses in contact with them very damp.'* He emphasises *'Their ruinous state and fearful overcrowding'* and sees *'no remedy for such property as this but removal.'* (p18)

Finally, he comments on the use of Corporation resources in addressing issues in this area:

'Mere Charity, which consists of only giving relief in money, in too many instances works more harm than good. It must be quite apparent to any person who has inspected the tenements in Wallace's-green, that no amount of money relief is of any avail in elevating and improving the condition of the recipients so long as they are left to crowd indiscriminately together, men, women, and children; the young of both sexes are educated in immorality, vice and crime. The cost of such structures can scarcely be named as objection to the cost of their reconstruction, seeing that little more than 1000/- would remove and rebuild, upon an approved plan, the whole property shown, equal to the accommodation of 30 families, or 150 persons. This would be better than expending 8000/- on a gaol for the accommodation of 12 prisoners – 9 male and 3 female – which has just been completed opposite to the property in question.' (p18)

At the time of the 1881 Census, a number of medical certificates were issued for those receiving outdoor Poor Law Relief. For the vast majority of women, this was for '*childbirth*,' whereas for men it was mainly for unspecified '*sickness*.' Both adults and children could be issued with medical certificates. The relief issued might take the form of milk for any children in the family, beef, mutton, bread, and flour. Certificates were issued to those across the Berwick-upon-Tweed Union but were more commonly provided to those living in the more impoverished and unsanitary areas of Berwick-upon-Tweed, such as Chapel Street, Hatter's Lane, Walkergate Lane, and Wallace Green.

Berwick-upon-Tweed Workhouse

The Guild and the Parish had the responsibility for the provision of the maintenance and the education of the poor. This was sometimes done jointly and sometimes separately. Relief usually took the form of small weekly payments, distributing the proceeds of the poor rate among those who were not able to provide for themselves.

The idea of establishing a House of Correction was first brought to the attention of the Guild in January 1654 (Scott, 1888). The necessity of '*putting idle persons to work*' was discussed and it was suggested that the Queen's Stables, situated near the Barracks, which had been granted to the Corporation by James I, could be used. At the time, the Queen's Stables were in the possession of the garrison and the consent of the Governor was applied for. A House of Correction was, therefore, established in 1657, following adaptation of the building, and a stock of spinning wheels was acquired to put people to task. The object of the House of Correction was to teach poor children to work. The implementation was, however, short-lived and the House of Correction was not supported further by the Guild and operation of the house was ended in 1661. The Guild attempted to sell the building but was unable to do so and it was eventually demolished in 1681. The site was used for the building of a vicarage.

The first workhouse in Berwick-upon-Tweed opened in July 1758 using a rented house in Church Street. Thirteen overseers were appointed to manage its operation. Paupers admitted to the Workhouse were tasked with teasing oakum for a local shipbuilder. Oakum is the name given to old tarry ropes. The task required paupers of the Workhouse to separate out the fibres of the ropes. The product of this process was used in caulking (sealing and waterproofing) the seams of planks in ships. Teasing oakum was not a pleasant task and was very hard on the fingers.

The Workhouse was originally planned to have 48 places, but quickly expanded beyond this number. In 1799, 47 of the 88 places available at the time were filled by children, who were taken in as a consequence of their parents being given relief. Around this time, approximately 300 people in total were in receipt of poor relief overall. A description of the Workhouse and its operation was given by Fuller (1799, p339-341):

'The State of the Poor'
'The house appointed for the reception of the poor of this Parish is situated near the upper part of Church-street. It consists of ten apartments, a kitchen, pantrys, besides a kitchen room for the keeper and his family. There is a room within the premises for the Overseers to hold their meetings in. Humanity and candour oblige us to confess that these lodgings are but ill adapted to the several conditions of the aged and infirm, as they are extremely cold in winter. This is owing to the buildings having suffered much from the ravages of time.
The beds are chaff laid on boards, with two or three pairs of blankets, and most of them are supplied with a coverlet. They have no curtains or other defence against the cold.
The regulations with regard to diet are as follows:
Beef or mutton and broth together with potatoe or cabbage pudding, and half a pound of wheaten bread for dinner two days per week.
Two days, potatoe broth made with suet, onions, etc. with bread, for dinner – for two days, a pint of table beer, with bread and a halfpenny worth of cheese or butter for dinner is each man's allowance a day. One day, new milk and barley boiled for dinner.
Pottage for breakfast with milk or small beer. Two days, bread and broth for supper, and the other five days pottage.
Clothing - The men and boys are clothed in thick blue woollen cloth, manufactured at Gallashiels in Scotland, and purchased in a shop in the town at 2s. 6d. per yard. The women's gowns are made of coarse cotton, called French Drogget, purchased at 1s.6d. per yard. Suitable aprons are purchased at the same price per yard.
The boys and girls are educated in reading and writing.
The women who choose to spin are allowed half of the profit. What is spun is wrought into coarse linen for shirts for the poor house.
There are at present 300 who receive charity from this institution. Forty-three are in the house; the remaining 257 live in the town and adjacent country; and are paid from one shilling and sixpence to two shillings, once a week.

> *The keeper of the house furnishes the poor lodged in it with victuals, coals and washing, for 2s. 4d. weekly, young and old. Besides he and his family having their lodgings free.*
> *There is a surgeon to attend both the house and such of the poor as are sick in the town.'*

NB – Poor rate at this time was 2 shillings in the pound.

This Workhouse building in Church Street was eventually replaced in 1803 using a building converted from a former sack factory in the High Greens area of the town. This was a larger building, better designed for its purposes, and included a school where pauper children could be educated by a Parish Schoolmaster. The building was later adapted in 1813, to create a new schoolhouse and a Lunatic Asylum, consisting of four cells. Thomas Johnston gives an account of the Workhouse at this time (1817, p106-109):

> *'Here the aged and infirm Children of poverty receive every attention, which their wants and condition require, and every regard is paid to their food and cleanliness. Here the poor and the helpless find a secure asylum from the miseries of want, and the evening of their day is spent, unclouded with temporal anxiety or distress.'*

Johnston further goes on to describe the functioning of the Workhouse:

> *'The Poor-House is under the direction of the Church Wardens, Overseers, and Trustees, who occasionally meet together to examine its internal management, and transact any business in which it is concerned. There are at present in the Poor-House upwards of 100 individuals, including 40 Children, under the immediate inspection of a House Governor, Schoolmaster, and Surgeon, by whom the most unwearied attention is paid to the health, morals, education, and comfort of those under their respective charge.*

The Children are instructed in Reading, Writing, and the Various Branches of Arithmetic, and at a proper age are sent out, the Girls to service, and the Boys as Apprentices to different Trades, as their friends or their own inclinations may direct.'

At this time, around 500 people were in receipt of some form of Parochial Relief. Johnston also makes reference in his account to the Lunatic Asylum where:

'the unhappy Maniac is attended to with all the humanity which his deplorable condition may require, and, at the same time, with all the vigilance necessary for the peace and security of Society.'

During this time, we begin to see the distinctions upon which medical diagnoses would subsequently be made. A distinction is made on functional grounds between the *'impotent'* poor, i.e. people not able to look after themselves, and the able-bodied. There is also the somewhat more moralistic distinction made between the *deserving* poor and the *undeserving* poor. This introduced an element of defining people who *should* be capable of working and supporting themselves from those who could not.

For many of us, the traditional image of a workhouse comes from Charles Dickens' *Oliver Twist*, first published in 1837. The images portrayed in the book clearly illustrate the austere and harsh nature of the regime of the workhouse. This is perhaps best remembered in the image of Oliver's starvation diet of thin gruel and the reaction he receives for politely asking for "more." In the Berwick-upon-Tweed Union Workhouse, however, there does seem to have been a reasonable attempt to keep things more humane. The Guild was central in providing support through local means in Berwick-upon-Tweed. That is not to say that conditions were ideal. Sanitation in the early 1800s was still very poor. Water supplies were still reliant on a system of wells throughout the town and contamination meant that the threat of cholera, in addition to other diseases, was always present.

Records do show, however, that Inmates of Berwick-upon-Tweed Workhouse were always well fed with a diet including regular portions of fish and meat twice a week as well as a staple diet of bread, oats, and milk. While the able-bodied were required to work, all children would receive a basic education. The provision of food, clothing, shelter, and medical care was available to all.

The images portrayed by Dickens were more likely to reflect conditions in large city-based workhouses, whereas smaller institutions were perhaps freer to operate more flexibly within their own local means.

Berwick-upon-Tweed Poor Law Union
Berwick-upon-Tweed Union was formally set up on the 21st November, 1836. It was overseen by an elected Board of Guardians representing the various Parishes in the area who were responsible to the Poor Law Commissioners in London. Parish areas covered by the Berwick-upon-Tweed Union were: Ancroft, Berwick-upon-Tweed, Cornhill, Duddo, Felkington, Grindon, Holy Island, Horncliffe, Kyloe, Loanend, Longridge, Norham, Norham Mains, Ord, Shoreswood, Spittal, Thornton, Tweedmouth, and Twizel. Berwick-upon-Tweed at the time had a population of 8,920, but the population of the total areas covered by the Workhouse was 20,782. The Workhouse was, from this time onward, no longer just for the Parish of Berwick-upon-Tweed alone, but served the wider Parish areas. Sheldon gives a description of the Workhouse: (1849, p318-319)

> 'The Poor House stands on the north-east side of Castlegate and was formerly used as a sack manufactory. The situation is healthy, and the building is fitted up in a most commodious manner. There are, on average, about 80 paupers, and 100 poor children receive education there. Connected with the poor-house is a Lunatic Asylum, built in 1813, containing four cells.'

'Besides the poor maintained in the Poor-house, there are upwards of 500 who receive parochial relief. The annual expense of the Poor-House and Lunatic Asylum amounts to upwards of £12,000, including the salary of the house governor, surgeon, schoolmaster etc.'

The Workhouse School

All Berwick-upon-Tweed children in receipt of poor relief were required to attend the Workhouse School. The school was also attended by children from the Parish. The new schoolroom was established in 1813. It was a single storey building erected on the north-west corner of the site, with one door and seven windows. At the time, around 100-120 children were taught in the school, of whom only about 30 would have been resident in the Workhouse (Cowe, 2018). Girls were taught sewing and boys worked in the garden. In terms of academic subjects, the Berwick-upon-Tweed Poor Law Union Minute Book of the 7th November, 1843, recorded that younger children were taught reading, spelling, and *'simple facts and maxims,'* while older children were taught, in addition, writing, arithmetic, geography, natural history, science, and religion (Cowe, 2018).

Although corporal punishment was used in schools at the time, there was a case on the 20th May, 1845, which reveals perhaps relatively progressive attitudes for the time. The case involved a situation where a child at the Workhouse School was left with marks on his hands following having been caned by a schoolmaster. This was investigated by the Guardians and a report was sent to the Poor Law Commissioners demanding the schoolmaster's immediate resignation. A letter of resignation followed and was accepted at the next Board of Guardians meeting held on the 1st July, 1845.

In 1855, there was some conflict between the Guardians and the Poor Law Board. Pressure was put on the Guardians for pupils to be educated in ordinary schools. The Guardians, however, retained the right of outdoor children to continue to be educated in the Workhouse School, and highlighted the advantages:

'In the Berwick-upon-Tweed Union outdoor pauper children in considerable numbers have attended the workhouse school for a long period. As this experiment, opposed as it is to notions long prevalent respecting the contaminating influence of a workhouse upon children, has been completely successful, and, as far as I know, has been attended by no evil consequences for 13 years at least, it appears to be especially deserving of notice, as many workhouse schools might receive outdoor pauper children in large numbers without any additional staff. The taint of pauperism does not seem to have been communicated in this case, and is probably not to be apprehended elsewhere as long as the demand for labour throughout the country is greater than the supply.' (from Cowe, p215)

The Revd Hamilton also pointed out other advantages of the Berwick-upon-Tweed system: 'We thus keep daily under good influence that very class from which criminal children and adult paupers are perpetually recruited' (from Cowe, p215). The school was, however, eventually closed and in 1869, 137 outdoor children started as pupils of the various schools in the area. On the 27th March, 1874 the Charity School Trustees commented that:

'the obsolete shape of the dress worn by some of the Workhouse children mark these children whilst at School, in an objectionable manner, and injurious to their future welfare.' (from Cowe, 2018, p219)

The 1881 Census

The 1881 Census, together with information from the Board of Guardians of Berwick-upon-Tweed Poor Law Union Minute Book, give us a good insight into what life was like for people categorised as 'Imbeciles' at the time.

The 1881 Census was collected on the 3rd April, 1881. The Census was a hand-written document and information was collected by an enumerator going door to door. Householders were asked to provide information about everyone who was at the property in question on that day. Householders were asked people's 'Name,' 'Relationship to Head of Family,' 'Condition as to Marriage,' 'Age,' 'Occupation,' and 'Where Born.' A final column recorded whether the person in question was (1) 'Deaf-and Dumb,' (2) 'Blind,' (3) 'Imbecile or Idiot,' or (4) 'Lunatic.'

The 1881 Census allows us to designate people in the Workhouse as belonging to one of four main categories: 'Children,' 'Non-Imbecile Adult Inmates,' 'Vagrants,' and 'Imbeciles.' 'Vagrants' were in the Workhouse as a result of the 1824 Vagrancy Act. There was a rise in homelessness and begging as a consequence of the end of the Napoleonic War and a downturn in the economy. The response in the 1824 Act was to make homelessness and begging illegal, thus requiring people to be housed overnight by the Parish. This also allowed people to receive a bath, a meal, and medical attention, if required. It served both as a mechanism to monitor and control aspects of public health as well acting as a deterrent to non-working in able-bodied people.

The term 'Imbecile' was used at the time to describe people who we would currently think of as having a mild to moderate intellectual disability. These are the people who would have traditionally carried out simpler, more menial tasks in society before the advent of mechanisation. The term 'Idiot' was used to define people with more severe disabilities. 'Imbecile' and 'Idiot' are now both used as terms of abuse, but their origins make them no different to the words we currently use to categorise people. In the 1800s, there was no formal measurement of peoples' level of ability and judgements were largely made on a functional basis, for example, by observation of what people were able to do on a day to day basis.

Children in the Workhouse were either orphaned or from families that were no longer able to support them, while the remaining group were largely elderly adults or widowed people who had lost the means to maintain their independence.

Board of Guardians of Berwick-upon-Tweed Poor Law Union Minute Book

The Board of Guardians Minute book gives some indication of the everyday operation of the institution, but it is a document of mainly administrative content. There are many references to the costs of running the Workhouse, for example, building repairs, improvements, and invoices from suppliers. The Workhouse received services from local butchers, bakers, grocers, spirit merchants, farmers, milk sellers, and undertakers. Accounts for supplies of bread, oatmeal, flour, milk, sugar, coffee, tea, rice, potatoes, butter, cheese, and bacon are listed. Improvements to conditions and practices are also discussed, for example, the minutes of the meeting held on the 5th May, 1879 note a *'desire to observe that the yard on the north side of the female imbecile ward will be improved as soon as the season permits the planting of some shrubs and flowers.'*

Poor Law Relief did not just pertain to people in the Workhouse. The majority of relief was given to people in the community. Around this time, approximately 500 other people in the Union area would also be in receipt of relief. Often reasons for incapacitation might be temporary and were the results of injury or illness. People in receipt of relief would be examined by medical staff and issued with a certificate describing the reason relief was being sanctioned. As well as a range of medical complaints, one common reason recorded for the issue of relief was *'childbirth.'*

There are a number of references to staffing issues, for example, appointments, promotions, and disciplinary matters. When Inmates of the Workhouse are named, this largely documents a transfer between Parishes or institutions, as this is when a cost would be involved. There is a regular reference to the number of *'pauper lunatics'* in the Northumberland County Lunatic Asylum and the cost thereof. On the 2nd June, 1879, for example, there is a minute about the death of Peter Flannigan in the County Lunatic Asylum who was *'one of the lunatics chargeable to this Union.'* Often, however, people were simply referred to by their category, as the main recorded concern of the Union was its finances. On the 29th December, 1879, the minutes read, '*the meeting were informed of the discharge from the County Asylum of three of the Pauper Lunatics chargeable to this Union and the death therein of another of such Lunatics.*'

County Lunatic Asylums

In 1845, the Lunacy Act was introduced. This legislation was administered by Commissioners in Lunacy. A '*Lunatic*' was defined as an '*insane person or any person being idiot or lunatic or of unsound mind.*' The establishment of the Royal Edinburgh Asylum in 1813 preceded the Lunacy Act and, prior to the establishment of the Northumberland County Lunatic Asylum in 1859, people from Berwick-upon-Tweed were likely to be placed there, as well as occasionally in institutions elsewhere.

The first indication of a working relationship between the Berwick-upon-Tweed Union Workhouse and the Northumberland County Lunatic Asylum is documented in the Minutes of the Board of Guardians on the 21st March, 1859, where a letter from William Dickson, Clerk to the Visitors of the new asylum states that '*the Pauper County Lunatic Asylum at Cottingwood, near Morpeth, was open for patients.*' William Dickson further writes on the 4th April, 1859, that '*only pauper lunatics chargeable to that part of the Union lying within the County of Northumberland could be accommodated at present.*' This is relevant, as some of the Parishes that formed part of the Berwick-upon-Tweed Union were located in the county of Durham at the time. This may explain why one of the people followed in this book was initially a patient in the Durham County Lunatic Asylum in Sedgefield, before being transferred to the Northumberland County Lunatic Asylum at a later date.

The Minutes of the Board of Guardians of the 3rd September, 1860 record that '*It was stated by the Royal Edinburgh Asylum that the charge, per annum, would be increased from £28 to £30 for each inmate. The inmates would, therefore, be removed to the County Asylum.*' Following this, as stated, all Berwick-upon-Tweed Union patients in the Royal Edinburgh Lunatic Asylum were moved to the new Northumberland County Lunatic Asylum in Morpeth.

The Northumberland County Pauper Lunatic Asylum
The Northumberland County Pauper Lunatic Asylum was established on the 16th March, 1859. It was visited by the Commissioners in Lunacy on a regular basis and was originally built to accommodate 200 male and female patients. This was the beginning of the growth of large, centralised institutions that placed people at a distance from their local communities. It was renamed the Northumberland County Mental Hospital in 1890 and later became St George's Hospital in 1937.

Male and female Inmates lived in separate wards in the Asylum and there was a ratio of at least one member of staff to every twenty-five patients. When patients were seen as being more difficult to manage, there was a ratio of at least one member of staff to every twelve patients. The grounds contained gardens, a chapel and a brewery. It was against the rules to hit patients or to keep them in perpetual restraint or seclusion. If a patient was restrained, it had to be reported to the Superintendent and documented in the Day Book as soon as was possible.

There was employment available during the day for both men and women. Men were able to work in the gardens and were taught trades by shoemakers, tailors, plumbers, and painters. Women were able to work in the laundry and the kitchen, as well as undertaking sewing, knitting, and mending work. Books were available and reading was encouraged. In the summer, men took part in sporting activities, such as cricket, bowls quoits, and football. Visits to the seaside for picnics also took place. Patients were well fed with a typical dinner consisting of meat, potatoes, bread, and beer. There was an emphasis on healthy living, recognising the importance of clean water, fresh air, and suitable occupation.

The Idiots Act of 1886

The equivalent institution, St Andrew's Colony, for people with an intellectual disability was not founded at Northgate, Morpeth until 1914, so people defined as 'Imbeciles' were more likely to be kept locally in the Workhouse up until that point. The Idiots Act was introduced in 1886 and dealt with establishing the educational needs of people with an intellectual disability. This act established a clear distinction between 'Lunatics' on the one hand and 'Idiots' and 'Imbeciles' on the other. Minutes of the Berwick-upon-Tweed Union, however, suggest that, in practice, this distinction had already been in place, with Inmates of the Workhouse having been categorised in this manner for some time. County institutions, however, represented a depersonalisation, decentralisation, and distancing of care from communities and systems of local support. Both institutions were built in the Morpeth area, around 45 miles away, not easily accessible for families from Berwick-upon-Tweed in those days.

Workhouse Staff

The Workhouse was staffed by a Master and a Matron, two Porters, a Girls' Attendant, and a Lunatic Attendant (see Table 1 below). It is of note that only one of the staff was born in the Berwick-upon-Tweed Union area. Staff lived on the premises with their families and children and it was not unusual for members of the same family to be employed together in the same facility.

Table 1: Workhouse Staff - 1881 Census

Name	Married	Age	Sex	Occupation	Birthplace
Rutherford, John	M	46	M	Workhouse Master	Hawick, Scotland
Rutherford, Hannah	M	50	F	Matron	Ripton, Durham
Rutherford, Sarah	U	20	F	Lunatic Attendant	Stocksfield, Northumberland
Morton, Elizabeth	U	25	F	Girls Attendant	Smeafield, Northumberland
Winton, Ellen	W	45	F	Nurse	Scotland
Scott, Robert	M	48	M	Porter	Twizel, Northumberland
Scott, Hannah	M	41	F	Porter	Hexham, Northumberland
Piscod, Isabella	N/A	3	F	Granddaughter	Consett, Durham

Note:
M = Married
U = Unmarried
W = Widowed

The Workhouse Layout

The Workhouse was designed with separate areas for different functions. Staff had their own quarters and there were separate facilities for men, boys, women and girls. Males were on one side of the building and females on the other. The building surrounded a series of four yards: The Men's Yard, The Boys' Yard, The Women's Yard and The Girls' Yard, where the Inmates went for fresh air and exercise. There was also a Stone Yard and a Sand Yard, where people worked. In respect of rooms within the buildings, new admissions to the Workhouse were screened and assessed in either the Men's or Women's Receiving Ward, while those who were only staying in the Workhouse overnight would be allocated to the male or female Vagrants' Ward, as appropriate. These were near a Bath House. There were also separate Day Rooms for men and boys. The health needs of the Inmates were tended to in the Hospital, while the children were educated in the School Room. The Workhouse Master had his own house and there was a Porter's Lodge. There was a Store, a Cellar, and a Coal House. Other facilities included a Dining Room, Wash Houses, and a Board Room. The Layout of the Workhouse can be seen in Figure 1 overleaf, taken from an 1852 Ordnance Survey Map.

Figure 1: *Berwick-upon-Tweed Union Workhouse from the Ordnance Survey Town Plan of Berwick-Upon-Tweed, surveyed 1852 (reproduced with the kind permission of the National Library of Scotland)*

Workhouse Inmates Listed in the 1881 Census

The Workhouse Inmates were people who could be categorised as belonging to one of four main groups: those classified as '*Vagrants*,' children, '*Imbeciles*,' and others. '*Vagrants*' were those who were brought into the Workhouse at night because homelessness and rough sleeping were illegal; children, for the purposes of this book, were those aged under 16, although they could work or be trained to work from the age of 12; '*Imbeciles*' were those who were viewed as lacking capacity to look after themselves, and the remaining Inmates were those who did not fall into any of the other categories.

At the time of the 1881 Census, there were 12 '*Vagrants*' in the Workhouse, all of whom were unmarried men from outside the Berwick-upon-Tweed Union area, with ages ranging from 18 to 58. All were listed as having been in occupations prior to entering the Workhouse.

There were 31 children living in the Workhouse, of whom 16 were boys and 15 were girls. Seven of the children were six years old or under, of whom two were babies. Twenty of the remaining children, aged 6 and over, were recorded as being '*Scholars*' (i.e. attending school), with the others having had occupations before entering the Workhouse.

There were 60 Inmates aged 17 or over in the Workhouse at the time of the Census – 30 were men and 30 were women. Five were married, 49 were widowed, and 14 were unmarried. Two people did not have their marital status recorded. Twenty-eight of the men (93%) and 13 of the women (43%) were recorded as having been in previous occupations before entering the Workhouse.

'Imbeciles'

In the Workhouse at this time there were 31 people categorised as '*Imbeciles*.' Only one was a child, aged 12 years old, named John Richardson. Twelve were adult men and 18 were adult women. Of the adults, the youngest was a female, aged 31. The oldest was a woman who was 78 years old. The majority (24) were from the Berwick-upon-

Tweed Union area, four were born in Ireland, one was from elsewhere in Northumberland, one was from elsewhere in England and it was not recorded where the other person was born. One of the men was married, one was widowed, and ten were unmarried. Four of the women were married, two were widowed, and 12 were unmarried. This indicates that 27% of those classified as *'Imbeciles'* were married or had been married prior to the death of their spouse. This is higher than recent figures gathered as part of one United Kingdom (UK) based study, between 2017 and 2018, which suggested only 5.5% of people with an intellectual disability were married/in a civil partnership, in comparison with 51% of the general population (McMahon et al., 2019).

Nine of the men were recorded as having occupations before entering the Workhouse – three were *'Farm labourers,'* three were *'General Labourers,'* two were *'Bakers,'* and one was a *'Butcher.'* Three did not have any previous occupation recorded. Seven of the women were recorded as having had occupations before entering the Workhouse – three were *'Field Workers,'* one was a *'Laundress,'* one was a *'Housemaid,'* one was a *'Boot Binder,'* and one was recorded as being a *'Schoolmistress.'* Eleven did not have any previous occupation recorded. Thus, of the 30 adults categorised as *'Imbeciles'* in the Workhouse, 75% of the men and 39% of the women had been in occupations before entering the Workhouse. These figures show that, overall, 53% had been in previous employment. This contrasts with current figures in the UK and Jersey of only 5.7% and 23% respectively (Hatton et al., 2018; McMahon et al., 2019).

Conditions of *'Imbeciles'* living in the Workhouse
In the Berwick-upon-Tweed Union Minute book, there is an entry on the 22nd of March, 1880, which contains a report from the Visiting Commissioners to Berwick-upon-Tweed Union Workhouse, dated the 16th February, 1880. This report specifically addresses the issues relating to the group of people categorised as *'Imbeciles'* at that time.

This is the year before the Census was taken and gives a good account of what conditions were like for people categorised as *'Imbeciles'* in the Workhouse at the time.

The account starts with a brief description of the visit and the number of the people categorised as *'Imbeciles'* the Commissioner talked to. He comments that the people he met did not require the care of an Asylum:

'I found my visit to this Workhouse today the names of 15 men and 16 women upon the list of imbecile paupers all of whom I have seen and spoken to and consider that they may all at the present time be properly cared for out of an asylum.'

The Commissioner then goes on to talk about the child who has been categorised as an *'Imbecile'*:

'There is one boy, John Richardson, who would undoubtedly be much benefitted by being sent to some idiot institution. He is now nine years of age and the Master informs me that he has improved since he has been in the house, that being the case, he is eminently likely to be able to be taught some useful trade.'

Reference is now made to the women in the Workhouse categorised as *'Imbeciles.'* The Commissioner talks of the paid nurse who is specifically employed to care for the more vulnerable and comments on her good credentials. He describes the living conditions of the women, making specific reference to sanitary problems experienced in the Workhouse. He also refers to the attempts made to plant shrubs in the yard to improve conditions, but he is not optimistic about their chances of success. These shrubs may refer to those mentioned earlier in recommendations for improvements made in the Berwick-upon-Tweed Union Minute of the 5th May, 1879:

'I saw all the women in the special wards and dormitories set apart for them under the charge of a paid nurse. She has been here for three years and seems, in all respects, a suitable attendant. These rooms were in good order and the beds and linen were clean and well attended to, but the whole of the WCs that I examined were either without a supply of water or the seat action out of order. A few shrubs have been planted in the back yard, but I fear they will not flourish.'

The Commissioner then makes comment on the conditions of the padded room used to contain violent patients. He describes it being in a quite dilapidated state. There are two possible interpretations about why the padded room is in such a state of disrepair. On the one hand, it could reflect a lack of care in the management of more difficult patients. On the other hand, it may be in a state of disrepair because of a lack of use:

'The padded room is quite unfit for a violent patient. The covering to the padding could be torn without the slightest difficulty. The padding itself is not sufficient and the nail fastening is objectionable.'

A further comment is made about the condition of the building:

'I would suggest also that the window in the skylight be made to open so as to afford increased means of ventilation.'

The Commissioner then goes on to talk about the plight of the male 'Imbeciles' in the Workhouse. He describes the work they do and the condition of the areas in which they are occupied. He reflects on the likely psychological impact of such conditions and recommends improvements:

'The male imbecile paupers are not nearly as well off. They are as herefore placed in a day room with other inmates. At my first visit there

26 men in the room engaged in cutting and tying up bundles of firewood. The room is long, narrow and dark. One of the three windows to the room was blocked by sacks of firewood stored at the end of the room, the other two windows look out onto a small airing court, which is the only court for the male patients, in which is placed the wood ready for chopping. There are no seats in it, and it presents by no means the appearance of a place likely to give enjoyment to anyone who went in it for exercise. But, dull as the court is itself, it is not as cheerful in appearance as the room above mentioned. The patients all sit on benches round the walls. The room is without chairs or tables and the sole ornament is one almanac stuck upon the bare walls. The room, in my opinion, is calculated to have a most depressing effect on the imbecile paupers who occupy it and I beg as strongly as I can to urge upon the Guardians the necessity of making some cheerful comforting appearance of the day rooms and to repeat the recommendations made by my colleagues on this score for several years past.'

The conditions in the Infirmary are addressed. He refers to the unsuitability of the bath and talks of impending improvements to the water supply:

'The infirmary bath might be improved as I hope it will. When the new water apparatus is set up by laying on hot water pipes and lowering the bath itself to the floor. At present, the patients have to mount 3 steps from the floor to get in the bath which must be awkward, if not positively dangerous, for the aged and infirm.'

The Commissioner refers to how the people categorised as *'Imbeciles'* in the Workhouse are clothed and fed. He also refers to how their spiritual needs are met:

'The dietary remains as before and is sufficient. From no-one did I hear any complaint. Both men and women were fairly well dressed and all have 2 suits of clothes or a change of dress. Divine Services are held by the Presbyterian Minister every Sunday evening.'

The Commissioner finishes his report with a statement endorsing the care received by people categorised as *'Imbeciles'* in the Workhouse: *'I think that the patients are very kindly treated.'*

Conclusion

This section charts the ways in which Berwick-upon-Tweed, with its unique position as *'County of a Town Corporate,'* enacted social policies in relation to poor relief. These practices included the categorisation of poor people, not only as *deserving* and *undeserving*, but also subsequently in terms of capacity and vulnerability. The Poor Law was originally designed as a system of welfare to keep impoverished people healthy, in order to ensure that there was a workforce at times of need. The desire to distinguish those who were *deserving* and *undeserving* of poor relief led to the initial categorisation. Subsequent policy and legislative changes were introduced in order to put the *undeserving* to work, while protecting the *deserving*. Medicalisation of the Poor Laws and the resultant change of emphasis in categorisation, further led to the growth of institutionalisation. People who had limited capacity ended up within a treatment model and eventually under a system that was designed to cure illness. The limits of the medical model in addressing social problems became evident as institutions rapidly expanded. In the next section we follow the lives of a group of people, who, through poverty, were forced to enter the Workhouse and subsequently were categorised as *'Imbeciles.'*

Making 'Imbeciles' of the Poor – Charting the Lives of People categorised as 'Imbeciles' in the Berwick-upon-Tweed Union Workhouse

As noted previously, the 1881 Census recorded 31 people living in the Workhouse who were categorised as 'Imbeciles.' Table 2 overleaf provides a summary of this group of people. While the report from the Visiting Commissioners concluded that the 'Imbeciles' were treated kindly, a number of areas of improvement of care were highlighted. This was, however, in a context where the living conditions of the poor who were receiving relief outside of the Workhouse were also harsh and unsanitary.

This section explores the personal histories of those who were categorised as 'Imbeciles' at the time of the 1881 Census, and, where possible, provides information about their lives before entering the Workhouse and charts their journey after 1881. Much of the information comes from the following main sources: Census records, the Berwick-upon-Tweed Poor Law Union Minute Book, and from the Northumberland County Archives – Record Books of St George's Hospital, Morpeth. The amount of information available varies from person to person and it is not always clear why a person has been classified as an 'Imbecile,' or in some cases an 'Idiot.' Today, an intellectual disability is defined as the person having significant impairments in cognitive functioning (an IQ less than 70) and in adaptive functioning, with onset in childhood (APA, 2013).

Table 2: *Inmates of the Berwick-upon-Tweed Union Workhouse categorised as 'Imbeciles' in the 1881 Census*

Name	Married	Age	Sex	Occupation	Birthplace
Arnott, Sarah	U	40	F		Murton
Bartram, William	U	64	M	Farm Labourer	Middle Ord
Brown, John	U	37	M		Goswick
Bryson, Christopher	W	65	M	Farm Labourer	Ord
Campbell, Matthew	U	34	M		Spittal
Campbell, George	U	40	M	General Labourer	Spittal
Christie, Margaret	W	78	F	Laundress	Berwick-upon-Tweed
Davidson, Fortune	W	76	F		Berwick-upon-Tweed
Dixon, Jane	M	51	F		Tweedmouth
Dumble, John	U	42	M	General Labourer	Tweedmouth
Fish, Jane	U	72	F	Boot Binder	Berwick-upon-Tweed
Flannigan, Ann	U	31	F	Field Worker	Ireland
Fogan, James	U	45	M	Farm Labourer	Scremerston
Gray, Maria	U	34	F		Ireland
Heslop, Jane	U	46	F		Berwick-upon-Tweed
Kerry, Mary A.	U	75	F		
Lovell, Patrick	M	66	M	General Labourer	Ireland

Name	Married	Age	Sex	Occupation	Birthplace
Mace, Isabella	U	45	F	House Maid Domestic Servant	Berwick-upon-Tweed
McNab, Elizabeth	U	42	F		Berwick-upon-Tweed
Morgan, Eliz.	M	31	F		Tweedmouth
Pringle, Charles	U	60	M		Woolwich, Kent
Richardson, John	Child	12	M		Scremerston
Robertson, Bridget	M	43	F		Ireland
Robertson, Thomas	U	40	M	Butcher	Berwick-upon-Tweed
Scott, Dorothy	U	38	F	Field Worker	Spittal
Spence, Philip	U	38	M	Baker	Tweedmouth
Todd, Margaret	U	49	F	Schoolmistress	Berwick-upon-Tweed
Trainer, Elizabeth	M	50	F		Berwick-upon-Tweed
Turnbull, Margaret	U	51	F	Field Worker	New Heaton, Cornhill
Whillis, Richard	U	33	M	Baker	Berwick-upon-Tweed
Wright, Jane Eleanor	U	49	F		Newcastle

Note:
M = Married
U = Unmarried
W = Widowed

Sarah Arnott

Sarah Arnott was born in Murton, a small farming settlement near Tweedmouth. In the 1841 Census, she is recorded as being two years old and living with her family in Campo. Her parents were John (32) and Elizabeth Arnott (30). She had five siblings living at that address: John (10), Margaret (8), Isabella (6), Joseph (4), and Elizabeth (5 months).

In 1851, she is recorded as living with her family at Shoreswood Farm, near Cornhill, south of the river Tweed. At that time, her father's occupation is listed as being a *'Master Blacksmith.'* Her father and mother are now aged 46 and 43 respectively. Her brother John (20) and her sister Margaret (18) are no longer living with the family. Her sister Isabella (16) is working as a *'Farm Servant.'* Sarah is now 12 years old and she and her siblings Joseph (13), Elizabeth (10), William, and Mary are all listed as *'Scholar.'* Although two siblings are no longer at home, there are three new additions: William (8), Mary (5), and David (3).

By 1861, the family are recorded as living in Kiln Hill, Tweedmouth. Her father, now aged 56, is working as an *'Engine Man.'* Sarah is one of three siblings still living at home, the other two being Isabella, who is now 26 and married, and David, who is just 13 years old. Although Sarah is 22 years old in 1861, she is not recorded as having any occupation and is unmarried.

In 1869, Sarah's father, John Arnott, dies at the age of sixty-five. In the 1881 Census, Sarah is recorded as being an Inmate of Berwick-upon-Tweed Union Workhouse. She is now 40, unmarried, and has no record of having previously been in an occupation. She is also now categorised as an *'Imbecile.'* Sarah Arnott dies in the Workhouse on the 25th July, 1884, aged 43.

Little is known about Sarah Arnott's life. It seems reasonable to conjecture, based on the limited information available, that she may have had an intellectual disability, as defined by current criteria. She lives with her family up until her father's death but does not appear to take up any occupation. She remains living at home with her parents as her siblings move on, away from the family. Her level of intellectual disability appears likely to have been mild, as she is recorded as being a '*Scholar*' as a child, suggesting she would have attended school.

She may have entered the Workhouse as the family were unable to continue to support her, following the death of her father. As Sarah had no occupation, she would have had to rely on her family for support. She would have become the responsibility of the Parish as family resources became overstretched. Entering the Workhouse under the categorisation of '*Imbecile*' would have both enabled the delivery of poor relief and allowed her to follow a regime more individually tailored to her capacity to function.

William Bartram

William Bartram was born in Middle Ord, a farming settlement near Tweedmouth, sometime around 1830. In the 1841 Census, he is recorded as living with his family in the Norham area. His father and mother are John (44) and Elizabeth Bartram (46). William is 11 years old at this time and lives with his six siblings: Elizabeth (19), John (15), Isabella (9), Hannah (6), Mary Ann (4), and Robert (2). In 1851, the family are living in Milfield, a small rural village near Wooler. William, now aged 21, is listed as being an *'Agricultural Labourer,'* the same occupation as his father, John (54), and his siblings Elizabeth (27), John (25), and Mary Ann (14). His siblings Isabella, Hannah, and Robert are not recorded as being at this residence in the 1851 Census. Agnes Younger (23) is listed as one of William's siblings, and is now living with the family with her four-month-old daughter, Elizabeth.

On the 24th January, 1859, William is admitted to the Durham County Lunatic Asylum. He was transferred to the Northumberland County Lunatic Asylum in Morpeth on the 1st August, 1859, aged 30. In the Asylum Relatives Address book his father, John Bartram, is listed as being his family contact. His father attempts to remove William from the Asylum, however, this was unsuccessful and on 23rd December, 1859, the Minutes of Board of Guardians of Berwick-upon-Tweed Union note that: *'It was reported that the request of Mr Bartram to remove his son (William Bartram) a pauper lunatic from the County Asylum had been refused.'* Less than a year later, on the 20th August, 1860, the Minutes note: *'In the County Asylum it was thought that William Bartram may be allowed to come out.'* Despite this, William is recorded as still being a patient in the County Lunatic Asylum in the 1861 Census.

A report by Dr Kirkwood on the 15th October, 1862, states that he is *'not fit to be discharged or removed to the Workhouse.'* A later report on the 14th September, 1863, from the Committee appointed to visit the County Lunatic Asylum states that: *'no favourable report can be made for the mental state of William Bartram.*' In 1866, William Bartram's father, John Bartram, dies aged 68.

William is recorded as residing in the County Lunatic Asylum in the 1871 Census. His age is recorded as being unknown, but his place of birth and previous occupation (noted in 1871 as having been a *'Farm Servant'*) is consistent with previous records. He is categorised in the 1871 Census as a *'Lunatic.'* The section of the admission records listing *'Name and Address of Relatives or Friends'* was left blank at the time of his second admission. William is discharged from the County Lunatic Asylum on the 23rd November, 1871.

Ten years later, William is recorded as being an Inmate of the Berwick-upon-Tweed Union Workhouse, where he is now categorised as an *'Imbecile.'* He is also categorised as an *'Imbecile'* in the 1891 and 1901 Censuses and he remains in the Workhouse throughout this period, until his death on the 4th May, 1910, aged 81.

It is unclear why William came to be categorised as an *'Imbecile,'* having been previously classified as a *'Lunatic.'* He came from a family of farm labourers and was admitted to the Northumberland County Lunatic Asylum while his father was still alive. William appears to have worked until his admission to the Durham County Lunatic Asylum in 1859. His father attempted, unsuccessfully, to have William discharged from Northumberland County Lunatic Asylum and it may be that the reason for the refusal of this request was that he was not capable of looking after William at this point in his life, through illness or injury. It may also have been that William was no longer able to function at the level required of a farm labourer, perhaps having previously worked with some help and assistance from others.

His admission to Northumberland County Lunatic Asylum, perhaps suggests some form of personal breakdown. His later transfer to the Workhouse and re-categorisation as an *'Imbecile'* also suggests that it may have been recognised that his difficulties were more to do with life-long impairments due to intellectual limitations, rather than a mental illness. He remained single throughout his life.

John Brown

John Brown was born in 1844 in Goswick. In the 1861 Census, he is recorded as being 16 years old and working as an *'Agricultural Labourer.'* He is living with his mother in East Kyloe, a small farming community to the south of Berwick-upon-Tweed. His mother, Elizabeth (56) is unmarried and a *'Farm Servant.'* On the 11th November, 1861, John's mother is admitted to the Northumberland County Lunatic Asylum. Ten years later, Census records show John, now 27, as being an Inmate in the Berwick-upon-Tweed Union Workhouse. He is categorised as an *'Imbecile from birth.'* The 1881 Census finds John still living in the Workhouse and categorised as an *'Imbecile.'*

John is admitted to the Northumberland County Lunatic Asylum on the 21st September, 1882, aged 38. He has no family or friends listed as contacts, he remained single throughout his life, and is described as having previously lived in the Workhouse for over 20 years. He is not listed as having any previous occupation and his *'Form of Mental Disease'* is listed as being *'Imbecility,' 'from infancy,'* the cause of which is *'Congenital.'* John dies in the County Lunatic Asylum on the 31st May, 1890. The cause of his death is listed as *'Acute Peritonitis.'*

John was born to an unmarried mother, who would have been approximately 40 years old when he was born. Working as a farm servant, she would not have had many resources of her own. Her admission to the County Lunatic Asylum is likely to have been the reason why John had to enter the Workhouse as she was no longer able to support him. His intellectual disability appears to have been apparent from childhood, although he seems to have been able to work as an agricultural labourer as a teenager, perhaps with some support from his mother.

Christopher Bryson

Christopher Bryson was born in Ord, a farming settlement near Tweedmouth, in 1811. The 1851 Census records him as being married and living in Front Street, Spittal, with his wife, Isabella (50). In 1851, Christopher (41) is listed as working as a *'Labourer,'* while Isabella's occupation is listed as *'Domestic Duties.'* In 1861, they are reported as living in Middle Street, Spittal, and Christopher's occupation is now listed as being an *'Agricultural Labourer.'* They also have a Lodger living with them, Thomas Bryson, who works as a *'Labourer at the Chemical Works.'* In 1871, they are living at Back Street, Spittal, and Christopher's occupation is listed as a *'Labourer.'* Ten years later, the 1881 Census records Christopher, who is now 72, as living in the Berwick-upon-Tweed Union Workhouse. He is listed as being widowed. We can, therefore, assume that Isabella must have died in the intervening years. His previous occupation is listed as an *'Agricultural Labourer'* and he is categorised as an *'Imbecile.'* Christopher died in the Workhouse on 10th March, 1889, aged 78.

Christopher Bryson seems to have been able to function quite adequately throughout most of his life. He was married and is recorded as having worked as a labourer for the majority of his life. It is unclear why he was categorised as an *'Imbecile'* later in life when residing in the Workhouse. It is possible that his wife was able to compensate for any shortcomings he may have had throughout his life and that he may not have had the capacity to cope on his own following her death. Other possibilities might relate to changes in Christopher himself that may have resulted from a head injury or an illness, such as dementia. In the 1800s, *'Imbecility'* was also used as a term to categorise those who had impaired intellectual capacity that could be as a result of a number of causes. It appears unlikely that Christopher would meet current criteria for intellectual disability as difficulties are required to have been present from childhood.

George and Matthew Campbell

George and Matthew Campbell (see Figure 2) were brothers who were both born in Spittal. George Campbell was born in 1841 and Matthew was born in 1848. In the 1861 Census, they are both living with their family in Spittal. Their father, John Campbell (49), is a *'Carter'* (road haulage using horses and carts) and their mother is Jane Campbell (48). George is 19 years old at that time and is also listed as being a *'Carter,'* along with his brother John, who is 15. Matthew is 13 and there is a younger sibling, James, who is four.

In the following Census in 1871, Matthew is living in the Berwick-upon-Tweed Union Workhouse. He is listed as being 23, unmarried, and is categorised as an *'Imbecile from 6 months.'* Ten years later Matthew, now aged 34, is still recorded as living in the Workhouse and his previous occupation is listed as being a *'General Servant.'* At this stage he is categorised as an *'Imbecile.'* He is joined in the Workhouse in 1881 by his brother George, who is aged 40 and unmarried. George's previous occupation is listed as being a *'General Labourer.'* He is also categorised at this stage as being an *'Imbecile.'*

In the 1891 Census, both Matthew and George are recorded as living in the Workhouse. Both are now categorised as *'Idiot from Childhood,'* implying lifelong difficulties. George's previous occupation is now listed as a *'Lamplighter.'* This change in recorded occupation might suggest that he has not been in the Workhouse consistently since the previous Census and that he may have worked in different roles when living outside the Workhouse.

Matthew is admitted to the Northumberland County Lunatic Asylum on the 23rd December, 1897, aged 49. He is not recorded as having any previous occupation, he is single, and his family contact is listed as being his brother, George, who is living in the Workhouse. Matthew's *'Form of Mental Disease'* is listed as being *'Idiocy'* and its cause is *'Congenital.'* He is noted as being dangerous to others *'at times when excited,'* but not suicidal or suffering from epilepsy.

In 1901, Matthew is recorded as still being a patient in the County Lunatic Asylum. He has no previous occupation recorded and is categorised as an *'Imbecile.'* There is some insight into Matthew's life in the hospital which can be gleaned from information in the County Lunatic Asylum Case Books. On the day of his admission his Medical Certificate states: *'He is an idiot. He is excitable. He cannot speak. He has been an inmate of the Workhouse for years, being certified an idiot.'* Matthew was also noted for both striking staff and other Inmates when in the Workhouse. The following day, the results of a physical examination describe him as follows: *'This patient is a little slight man with a small pointed face and a childish expression. Hair white, eyes grey.'* His mental condition is reported as: *'He seems idiotic and it is impossible to make out what he says. He seems to understand what is said to him as he obeys promptly when told to do something.'*

At some point he is assigned work in the *'outdoor squad'* and on the 4th January, 1998, is noted as being *'Quite demented but quiet and not at all troublesome.'* There is little of note throughout 1898, with the records frequently reporting *'No change.'* He is perceived as being content by the staff, who note that he *'Continues to work with outdoor squad,'* and that he is *'healthy,'* and *'happy.'* An examination and a *'Special Report'* on the 23rd November, 1898, give an idea of Matthew's abilities, as assessed at the time: *'He labours under idiocy. He cannot answer the simplest questions. He assents to anything e.g. that he is 10 years of age, that 6 is only one and that he is 10 feet in height.'* This picture is unchanged throughout 1899, with Matthew being described consistently as someone who is unable to speak and with severe cognitive difficulties. In April that year, he is described variously as: *'This idiot has no intelligence – cannot speak and makes weird noises in attempts to answer questions'* and *'This little stunted idiot is without intelligence. He cannot speak.'* The aggressive tendencies that were reported on his admission appear not to have been present at that point in his life. On the 25th April, 1899, he is described as unchanged and *'a simple good-tempered little fellow showing only little intelligence. He works with the outdoor squad,'* while on the 21st

July that same year: '*Unchanged – Quite harmless – Useful in Farm and Garden.*' Reference was also made to his physical appearance, being described on the 14th October, 1899, as: '*This dwarfish idiot has no intelligence. He cannot speak.*'

Assessment of ability appeared to be rudimentary, with attempts to engage the patient in conversation and to ask questions such as the person's age. Measures of physical health, such as respiration and temperature were also taken. Matthew was considered to perform poorly in respect of his cognitive abilities and in November 1899, it is reported that: '*Patient is an idiot. He is incapable of rational conversation. When asked how old he was he held up two fingers.*' Matthew's Continuation Certificate concluded that: '*He labours under idiocy. Has practically no intelligence. He says he has two fingers and two noses. Resp. 24, Temp. 96.6.*'

Between February and April 1901, Matthew suffered from bowel problems and was in the infirmary for treatment. It was reported that the problem was resolved and that he made a full recovery. He continued to be compliant, good natured, and to work in various roles, including the responsibility of looking after the doctor's chickens. In July 1901, it was noted that: '*This little man is quite unchanged. He looks after the Doctor's hens. He is very quiet and easily managed.*' In October, he worked in the gardens: '*This dwarf does a little work in the garden around No1 Villa. He is very childish and cannot speak intelligibly. He is quiet and very good natured.*' Perhaps it is illustrative of the settled, routine nature of Matthew's life that the notes following that period indicated no change until his death in 1917. In October 1906: '*This idiot remains mentally and bodily unchanged,*' in January 1907: '*In every respect unchanged,*' and in April, 1910: '*This congenital case shows no change.*' Matthew dies in the County Lunatic Asylum on the 21st June, 1917. His cause of death is listed as '*Senile Decay.*'

By contrast to his brother, the 1901 Census records George, at the age of 58, to be back living in Spittal with his younger brother, John, and working as a '*Labourer.*' The 1911 Census records George as living

Figure 2: *Image of Matthew Campbell from the Northumberland County Lunatic Asylum Records - Male Chronic Case Book (NRO 03680/234). Reproduced with kind permission from the Northumberland County Archives.*

as a Lodger in Chapel Street, Berwick-upon-Tweed. He is 69, single and working as a '*General Labourer.*' The date and cause of his death are unknown.

It would appear that Matthew was the less able of the two brothers and spent more time in institutional care throughout his life. Matthew seems to have benefitted in some ways from the institutional care provided by the County Lunatic Asylum. His behaviour was described as previously being challenging in the Workhouse, where he was recorded as striking staff and others. In the County Lunatic Asylum, by contrast, he is noted as being '*harmless,*' '*not at all troublesome,*' '*happy,*' '*useful,*' and '*very good natured.*' This difference may be due to Matthew consistently having work to do that was within his capabilities. These jobs also may have given him a sense of being valued, for example, looking after the doctor's hens and working in the farm and garden.

George seems to have required assistance only at specific periods of his life and was able to move on from requiring the assistance of the Workhouse. He returns to living with family and resumes employment later in life. For George, the Workhouse appears to have provided intermittent support at times of particular need, so his intellectual limitations are unlikely to have been anything more than mild. Matthew's notes, however, describe someone with more marked intellectual impairment, with additional communication difficulties, and the physical characteristics of someone who might today be diagnosed with a specific syndrome.

Margaret Christie

Margaret Christie was born in Berwick-upon-Tweed in 1803. In the 1841 Census, she is 35 and recorded as living with her husband, David Christie (45), in Hatter's Lane, Berwick-upon-Tweed. Her husband was previously a soldier in the Army and the 1851 Census records them as living off David's army pension, in Marygate, Berwick-upon-Tweed. Margaret's occupation is listed as a *'Dressmaker.'* In the 1861 Census, they have moved back to Hatter's Lane. Ten years later, Margaret is recorded as being an Inmate of the Berwick-upon-Tweed Union Workhouse. She is now 68 years old and is listed as being widowed. It is not until the 1881 Census, that Margaret, now 78, is categorised as an *'Imbecile,'* with her previous occupation being listed as a *'Laundress.'* Margaret dies in the Workhouse on the 16th January, 1883, aged 80.

The records show Margaret as living with her husband for most of her life and she is only required to enter the Workhouse following being widowed. The couple had, up until this time, lived off her husband's army pension. In the mid-1800s, however, a woman would not have had an entitlement to her husband's pension following his death. As a widow, Margaret would have had to rely on poor relief if she had no significant resources of her own. Entering the Workhouse would have ensured she was supplied with the basic necessities of life, such as food, clothing, and accommodation.

It is of interest that she is not listed as an *'Imbecile'* in the 1871 Census but is in the later 1881 Census. It could be that her disability was mild and was not initially evident on entering the Workhouse, following her having lived a somewhat protected existence with her husband up until his death. It could also be that this categorisation represented a change in her condition in later life, for example, as a result of dementia, rather than reflecting an intellectual disability.

Fortune Davidson

Fortune Davidson was born in Lowick in 1805. In the 1841 Census, she is recorded as living in Kiln Hill, Tweedmouth, with her husband and children. Her husband, Charles (40) was a *'Shepherd'* at that time. Fortune is 36 years old and the couple have five children living at home: Jane (16), Charles (11), James (8), Andrew (6), and Robert (1). Ten years later, the family are still living in Kiln Hill, although her husband is now a *'Labourer.'* Six children are now living with the family, with her son Thomas (18), also being recorded as living at home. The eldest daughter Jane, is not recorded as having any occupation, while Charles is working as a *'Labourer,'* Thomas and Andrew are both *'Apprentices,'* and Robert and Eleanor are *'Scholars.'*

In 1857, Fortune's husband dies aged 56. Four years later, the 1861 Census records Fortune as head of the household and as still living in Kiln Hill with her three sons: Charles, a *'Moulder'* who is widowed, Andrew, a *'Blacksmith,'* Robert, a *'Joiner,'* and her daughter Eleanor, who is still a *'Scholar.'* No record could be found of Fortune in the 1871 Census, however, in 1881 she is recorded as being an Inmate of the Berwick-upon-Tweed Union Workhouse. At this point she is 76 and is categorised as an *'Imbecile.'* Fortune died in the Workhouse on the 10th December 1882, aged 77.

Fortune lived with her husband and family for the main part of her life and only entered the Workhouse in the latter years of her life. She kept the family together as head of the household following her husband's death. It is possible that she had intellectual difficulties throughout her life and was only able to live in Kiln Hill with the support of her family. It seems more likely, however, that there was a change in her condition in her later years, possibly as a result of dementia or some other form of infirmity and that the category of *'Imbecile'* was used to represent the later decline in her cognitive and functional abilities.

Jane Dixon

Jane Dixon was born in Tweedmouth in 1830. In 1851, the Census recorded her as living with her family in Tweedmouth under her maiden name, Jane Waters. At that time, she is 19 years old and a *'Servant.'* She is living with her father, Adam Waters (62), a *'Mariner,'* her mother, Margaret Waters (52), and her married sister, Elizabeth Hogan (27), who is listed as a *'Soldier's Wife.'* Ten years later, Jane remains living in Tweedmouth with her father, who is now widowed and a *'Pensioner,'* and her sister. Her sister is now referred to as Elizabeth Waters, as unmarried, and her occupation is a *'Housekeeper.'* In the interim, Jane has married and is referred to as Jane Dixon, with a listed occupation of a *'Plasterer's Wife.'*

In the 1871 Census, Jane is recorded as living in Main Street, Tweedmouth, with her father, who is now 82 and a *'Pensioner,'* and her husband. Jane is a *'Housekeeper,'* while her husband, William Dixon (34), is a *'Plasterer.'* Her husband was the son of William Dixon, also a plasterer, and Mary Ann Dixon (nee Crosby), from the Castlegate area of Berwick-upon-Tweed.

Later in 1871, Jane's father dies at the age of 82 and three years later her mother in law dies, aged 63. In 1881, the Census records Jane, now 51 and still married, as being an Inmate of the Berwick-upon-Tweed Union Workhouse. There is no previous occupation listed for her and she is categorised as an *'Imbecile.'* Also living in the Workhouse at this time is Jane's father-in-law, William Dixon, who dies a year later, aged 73.

Jane was admitted to the Northumberland County Lunatic Asylum on the 7th May, 1881. On admission, she is listed as being the wife of William Dixon, *'Plasterer'* and her home address is 87 High Street, Berwick-upon-Tweed. Her *'Form of Mental Disease'* is listed as *'Delusional Insanity'* and it is recorded as having been present for eight years prior to the date of admission. Jane died in the County Lunatic Asylum on the 9th August, 1885, aged 55. Following her death, in the

1891 Census, Jane's husband William Dixon is recorded as working as a '*Servant*' for his relatives, the Edgar family, in Berwick-upon-Tweed.

Jane lived for most of her life with her family. Her father had a pension and this would have allowed her to have functioned as his housekeeper. This suggests that any intellectual impairment she may have had was mild. She was married and her husband worked as a plasterer, but she entered the Workhouse following her father's death, suggesting her father may have been her main source of support. She appears to have had long-standing mental health difficulties, which may have been the trigger for her admission to the Workhouse and her subsequent transfer to the County Lunatic Asylum, rather than an intellectual disability.

John Dumble

John Dumble was born in Tweedmouth in 1839. In 1851, the Census records him as being 15, a *'Pauper,'* and a visitor of Mary Hogg (44), an unmarried woman with no listed occupation, who lives in Back Street, Spittal, with her daughter Margaret (18), a *'Servant.'* In the following Census, John is a lodger in Middle Street, Spittal, with Robert Emery (63), who works as a *'Labourer in Iron Foundry.'* John is unmarried and his occupation is listed as being a *'Common Labourer.'* Also living as a lodger at this property is Mary Hogg, who is still unmarried, but now working as a *'Dressmaker.'*

Ten years later in 1871, John is still living as a lodger with Mary Hogg, but they are now in Middle Street, Spittal, along with Francis Mary Gilbert (9), who is a *'Scholar.'* John is now 37, unmarried, and his occupation is listed as being a *'Labourer in Ironworks.'* Mary Hogg remains unmarried and a *'Dressmaker.'* In 1881, John is an Inmate of the Berwick-upon-Tweed Union Workhouse. His previous occupation is listed as being a *'General Labourer,'* and he is categorised as being an *'Imbecile.'* John died in the Workhouse on the 12th November, 1890, aged 51.

It seems likely that there was some connection between John and Mary Hogg. He is recorded from the age of 15 as being with Mary and remains lodging with her over subsequent years until he is admitted to the Workhouse. It is possible that Mary died prior to John's admission, as there was no record of her in the 1881 Census. While John was able to work as a *'Labourer'* throughout his life, he may have been unable to cope without Mary's support. Any intellectual impairment he may have had is likely to have been mild.

Jane Fish

Jane Fish was born in Berwick-upon-Tweed in 1809. She is recorded in the 1841 Census as having no occupation and as living in Marygate, Berwick-upon-Tweed, with her father, John (60), a *'Shoemaker,'* her mother, Ann (55), and siblings John (30), a *'Boot Maker,'* Samuel (25), who has no occupation listed, James (25), a *'Boot Maker,'* Joseph (20), a *'Cabinet Maker,'* and Alex (15). It appears that Jane was one of triplets, with the next Census also recording a sister Eleanor, who was the same age as Jane and her brother John. The family also appears to have a set of twins – Samuel and James.

In 1851, Jane is still living with her family in Marygate, although her father no longer appears in the Census. Her brother John, now a *'Master Boot Maker,'* employing 22 men, has assumed the role of head of the family. Also living at home are Jane's mother, her brothers Samuel, also a *'Master Boot Maker,'* and James, a *'Boot Maker,'* and her sister Eleanor. Both Jane and Eleanor, two of the triplets, have no occupation listed.

At some point, Jane and Eleanor move to the High Street, Berwick-upon-Tweed, where Jane is recorded as being head of the household in 1861. Both are now 52 and they are listed as having the occupation of *'Laundress.'* Her brother Joseph (40), a *'Cabinet Maker,'* his wife Elizabeth (38), and their son, Joseph (7), a *'Scholar,'* live in the property next door.

In the 1881 Census, Jane, now 72, is recorded as being an Inmate of the Berwick-upon-Tweed Union Workhouse. She is listed as being unmarried and as having previously had the occupation of *'Boot Binder.'* She is categorised as an *'Imbecile.'* Jane dies in the Workhouse, a year later, on the 29th August, 1882.

Jane is first recorded as having an occupation (*'Launderess'*) in the 1861 Census, when she was in her fifties. She remained single throughout her life and lived with or near family members prior to her admission to the Workhouse. Although recorded as head of the household when she and Eleanor lived together, it seems likely that she relied on her family for support. It is possible that, in later life, this support fell away, and she was no longer able to cope on her own, resulting in admission to the Workhouse. She appears to have been one of triplets, which carries with it an increased chance of experiencing intellectual difficulties (Moore & O'Brien, 2006), for example, due to the increased risks of prenatal and birth complications. Alternatively, it may only have been in later life that she was unable to cope due to, for example, illness or dementia, rather than intellectual disability.

Ann and Jane Flannigan

Ann Flannigan is listed as having been born in Ireland, sometime around 1850, but it is also possible that she was born in Berwick-upon-Tweed, the daughter of an Irish immigrant. In the 1851 Census, she is recorded as living with her family in Walkergate Lane, Berwick-upon-Tweed. Her family comprises her father, Arthur (35), who is Irish, head of the household and a *'Labourer,'* his wife, Ann (33), who is from Berwick-upon-Tweed, her sisters Mary (13), Margaret (8), and brother George (2 months), all of whom were born in Berwick-upon-Tweed. Also living with the family was Mary Doherty (68), who was a servant, born in Ireland.

A report by Dr Kirkwood, Medical Officer, on the 17th January, 1853, states that Ann's father, Arthur Flannigan had been admitted to the Workhouse *'in an insane state.'* It was suggested by Mr Christison, of the Board of Guardians, that Arthur Flannigan be *'removed to a lunatic asylum.'* It was also debated whether he should be returned to his then perceived place of settlement in Scotland. On the 16th June, 1856, however, Arthur Flannigan (43), is at home in Hatter's Lane, Berwick-upon-Tweed, where he is in receipt of a medical certificate for *'nervous debility'* and is *'prescribed bread and oatmeal.'* On the 27th July, 1857, the Board of Guardians Minutes note a further medical certificate recorded for Arthur Flannigan, of Hatters Lane, *'for insanity.'* He is *'prescribed necessaries'* and the certificate is signed by Dr Kirkwood. On the 10th August, 1857, Dr Kirkwood issues a medical certificate for Arthur Flannigan, *'aged 43, labourer, of Hatters Lane, Berwick, for insanity'* and he is, again, *'prescribed necessaries.'* On the 3rd May, 1858, Dr Fluker issues a medical certificate for Arthur Flannigan *'for insanity'* and he is *'prescribed necessaries.'*

The 1861 Census finds the family living at Walkergate Lane, although Ann's widowed grandmother, Mary Wilson (94), is now head of the household. She is listed as being a *'Pauper Cook'* who was born in Berwick-upon-Tweed. Ann's mother is now recorded as being unmarried and a *'Pauper.'* Ann's sisters, Mary and Margaret, are no longer reported as living with the family, however, her brother George and a new baby brother Arthur (1) are living with her.

In 1871, Ann is recorded as living as a *'Lodger'* with the Wilson Family at 25 Silver Street, Warrington, Lancashire. The family comprise Edward Wilson (30), head of the household, with no recorded occupation, who is Irish and married to Mary (27), also born in Ireland. They have two children, John (4) and Peter (1). As well as Ann, they also have a Mary Flannigan (61) lodging with them, who was Irish, with no recorded occupation. It is likely, but not confirmed, that the Flannigan and Wilson families were related.

It is unclear when Ann returned to Berwick-upon-Tweed, but she gives birth to her daughter, Jane Flannigan (see Figure 3), in the Berwick-upon-Tweed Union Workhouse on the 24th July, 1880. There is no record in the Workhouse documents of who Jane's father was. Ann appears in the 1881 Census with her 8-month-old child, Jane, in the Workhouse. Ann, then 31, is categorised as being an *'Imbecile.'* She is recorded as having previously worked as a *'Field Worker.'* Ann and Jane both appear again in the Workhouse in the 1891 Census, aged 41 and 10 years old respectively. Ann is categorised as an *'Idiot from Childhood.'* Ann died in the Workhouse on the 9th December that same year.

Jane remains in the Workhouse until the 5th April, 1894, when at the age of 13, she is placed at St Catherine's Convent, Lauriston Gardens in Edinburgh. Five years later, on the 12th October, 1899, Jane is admitted to the Northumberland County Lunatic Asylum. She has no previous occupation listed and the section of her notes titled *'Name and address of Relative or Friends'* is filled in with the single word – *'None.'* Her *'Form of Mental Disease'* is listed as being *'Imbecility'* which is *'Hereditary'* and present *'since birth.'* She is noted, on admission, as not being epileptic, suicidal, or dangerous to others. Some further insight into Jane's condition at admission is provided by her Medical Certificate which notes:

> 'She is constantly clasping and unclasping her hands, is very restless – Moving and looking around furtively in an aimless fashion.'

Her appearance and interactions were described negatively:

> 'She is dirty and uncleanly in her habits, is often subordinate without any reason and deliberately often does the opposite of what she is told. She is incapable of being taught. Her mother was an imbecile.'

In terms of her mental state, Jane is described as follows:

> 'Patient doesn't know the month of the year or how long she has been where she is or why she was sent here. Is very backward in education. Cannot add the simplest figures. Talks in a childish simple way.'

A few days later, on the 16th October, 1899, she is reported as being in good physical health and her *'Imbecility'* is confirmed:

> 'She labours under imbecility. She talks in a simple childish way and as a rule is unable to answer the simplest questions e.g. her own age.'

Jane is set to work in the laundry. In the 1901 Census, Jane is still in the County Lunatic Asylum, categorised as an *'Imbecile.'* Between October 1899 and July 1901, Jane's notes simply record a series of entries reporting *'no change'* in her condition. On the 22nd July, 1901, some further detail is provided, with Jane being described as:

> 'This imbecile is mentally unchanged. She is very simple and has a foolish manner. She is somewhat hilarious and knows nothing. She does a little work – is in good general health – clean in her habits – eats and sleeps well – weighs 100 lbs.'

This is again followed by a period of entries reporting no change in

Figure 3: *Image of Jane Flannigan from the Northumberland County Lunatic Asylum Records - Female Chronic Case Books (NRO 03680/278) Reproduced with kind permission from the Northumberland County Archives).*

Jane. On the 9th July, 1902, there is some suggestion of a deterioration in her behaviour:

> 'No mental improvement in this idiot – She is sometimes noisy and troublesome and often mutters away to herself the whole day.'

Her work pattern becomes erratic, with the records noting in October 1902, that she has stopped working:

> 'This imbecile remains as childish and stupid as ever. She cannot carry out any sort of conversation. She laughs in a silly manner when spoken to. She does no work of any sort.'

By contrast, on the 29th January, 1903, she is described as undertaking some work, but continuing to display behaviour that the staff found challenging:

> 'No change in this imbecile – does a small amount of work in Ward VII. Is often very difficult to manage. In good health.'

On the 10th April, 1903, she has resumed work in the laundry and appears to be less problematic from a staff perspective:

> 'This imbecile remains unchanged. She is now working in the laundry. Is quiet. Has a good appetite. Sleeps well.'

Her Continuation Certificate dated the 12th September, 1903, notes:

> 'She labours under imbecility. She is childish in manner and speech. She has no idea of time or number. She cannot tell how many fingers she has. She cannot tell how long she has been here.'

Little change in Jane is noted throughout the rest of 1903. She continues to work in the laundry and her physical health is reported as being good. In 1904, there are again a number of entries reporting that she is noisy and difficult:

29th January, 1904 – *'This very noisy patient works well in the laundry and is unchanged. Mentally and physically – health good.'*

Her difficult behaviour is frequently noted alongside her ability to work well:

13th April, 1904 – *'This patient works in the laundry. She is sometimes very abusive and noisy though generally a good worker. Weight 106lbs.'*

Her mental health appears to continue to deteriorate throughout 1904 and 1905 and she becomes aggressive. She seems to suffer from auditory delusions at times:

4th October, 1904 – *'This patient becomes very excitable and tears her clothes at the menstrual periods. She fights the wall and hears voices. She works well in the laundry.'*

19th January, 1905 – *'This woman is extremely excitable, but she works well in the laundry. She eats and sleeps well.'*

In May 1905, she is reported as experiencing some physical health problems, including enlargement of glands in the neck and problems with abscesses in her mouth due to *'several decaying teeth.'* On the 12th July, 1906, the staff report:

'This patient is quite imbecile. She does not know how long she has been here nor the name of this place, nor the month or year. She

does a little work in the laundry but still runs about a great deal. Her bodily health is good. Wt. 105lbs.'

Two months later, on the 11th September, 1906, her Continuation Certificate confirms her *'Imbecility'* and good physical health. The doctor seems particularly surprised that Jane reports never having heard of Jesus Christ, perhaps because of the time she spent in St Catherine's Convent prior to her admission to the County Lunatic Asylum:

'She labours under imbecility. Her mental powers are very limited. She states that she has never heard of Jesus Christ! Says that 3 X 3 are 6. Bodily condition is good. Body clean, well-nourished and believed to be free from injury. Appetite good, pulse 56, resp 18, temp 98°.'

Again, on the 9th February, 1907, the same picture of Jane's condition is painted in the notes:

'This patient cannot answer the simplest question correctly. She says she has 7 fingers, cannot tell how many toes she has as her boots are on. She cannot tell where she is nor how long she has been here. She is fairly tidy in her habits. Works in the laundry. Is in good bodily health. Eats and sleeps well, weight 105lbs.'

On the 28th April, 1909, the notes describe Jane as suffering from extreme mood swings:

'Patient is mentally unchanged. Is sometimes maniacal. Habits are clean and tidy. Works in laundry. Health good.'

This is repeated on the 13th September, 1909:

'Patient is mentally unchanged. Is sometimes maniacal. Habits are clean and tidy. Works in laundry. Health good.'

Despite this, there is no mention of this in the Continuation Certificate dated that same day:

> 'She labours under imbecility, her personal intelligence is very limited. She does not know where she is or how long she has been here. She cannot tell the day, month or year. Bodily condition poor. Body clean, poorly nourished and believed to be free from injury. Heart and lungs normal. Appetite good. Pulse 60, Resp 16. Temp 97.4°.'

Between this time and 1914, the notes report little change in Jane. On the 18th September, 1914, there is some indication of cognitive decline, with a reduction in her work and loss of speech:

> 'This imbecile is in good health. Clean in her habits and works a little in the laundry. Has no intelligence and does not speak even when spoken to.'

The decline continues, with Jane being described as demented for the first time on the 20th July, 1916:

> 'Is demented, does only very little sewing in the ward.'

...and again, on the 14th November, 1918, with little of substance reported in the notes in the interim years:

> 'Demented and childish. Does some work in the laundry.'

Later, a Special Report notes that:

> 'She is labouring under imbecility. Her intelligence is much impaired, she cannot answer simple questions, she does not know her age, the day, the month, or year. Bodily she is fair. Body fairly nourished, clean and free from injury. Breath sounds harsh. Heart action normal, T 97.2° R 20.'

There is little else substantive recorded in the notes about Jane's life between this time and 1919 (which marks the end of the period of time where her notes were publicly available for study). Jane died in the County Lunatic Asylum on the 25th May, 1924, aged 44.

Jane was born and lived her life in institutions. She was born in the Workhouse, spent some time in a Convent and lived her adult life in a County Lunatic Asylum. Her mother, Ann, entered the Workhouse when she was pregnant with Jane, having had some previous employment as a *'Field Worker.'* Jane has no recorded father and her mother died in the Workhouse when Jane was only ten years old.

It is unclear whether Ann's categorisation as an *'Imbecile'* reflected a lack of intellectual capacity or whether it was applied because she was an unmarried mother of Irish origin, with no means to support herself. There is, however, much clearer evidence that Jane had lifelong intellectual impairment. While she was able to carry out basic work in the County Lunatic Asylum, there is also evidence of longstanding disturbed behaviour. Her notes describe her as someone who had additional mental health difficulties. These would be further compounded by a lack of family attachments and the long-term effects of institutionalisation.

James Fogon

James Fogon was born in Scremerston in 1836. In the 1881 Census, when he is 45, James is recorded as being an Inmate of the Workhouse. He is unmarried and listed as having a previous occupation as a *Farm Labourer.* He is categorised as an *'Imbecile.'* He is still in the Workhouse at the time of the 1891 Census and at this point he is categorised as an *'Idiot from Childhood.'* James dies in the Workhouse on the 26th December, 1891, aged 55.

It was difficult to find any other verifiable information about James' life. Although he is recorded as having had previous employment, the work is likely to have been unskilled. He is later listed as being an *'Idiot from Childhood'* suggesting he would have had significant intellectual difficulties. It may be that he entered the Workhouse following a loss of family support.

Maria Gray

Maria Gray was born in 1845 in Antrim, Ireland. At some point between her birth and 1861 her family travelled to Berwick-upon-Tweed as the 1861 Census records them as living in the Greenses area. The family comprises her father, William (57), a *'Coastguardsman,'* her mother, Rachael (56), her sister, Susanna (19), and her brother Joseph (17). Neither of her siblings are married or listed as having any occupation. Maria is 14 at the time and a *'Scholar.'* Both of her parents are recorded as having been born in Berwick-upon-Tweed, but all three children were born in Ireland, suggesting her father may have worked there in the past.

Ten years later, the 1871 Census finds the family still living in the Greenses area. Her father, who is now 67, is a *'Pensioner.'* Neither Maria or her sister Susanna have an occupation listed and both are unmarried. William (6), who is the nephew of Maria's parents, is also in the household.

In the 1881 Census, Maria is recorded as being an Inmate of the Berwick-upon-Tweed Union Workhouse. She is unmarried, has no previous occupation, and is categorised as an *'Imbecile.'* The 1891 Census finds Maria still an Inmate of the Workhouse. Her previous occupation is now noted as being a *'General Servant.'* She is categorised as an *'Idiot from Childhood.'* Maria is recorded as present in the Workhouse in the 1901 and 1911 Censuses and remains unmarried and categorised as an *'Imbecile'* during these periods. In 1911, she is noted as having had a previous occupation as a *'Bottle Washer in a Chemist.'* Maria dies on the 2nd January, 1914, in the Workhouse, aged 69.

Maria lived with her family for the early part of her life and her father would have had a regular income from his pension. It seems likely that she would have entered the Workhouse sometime after her father's death, as this would have represented both a loss of support and a loss of income. Maria appears to live the rest of her life in the Workhouse, probably unable to move on because of her lack of capacity to support herself. Her sister, Susannah, marries James Simpson and continues to live in Berwick-upon-Tweed. The couple have three children and Susanna dies in Berwick-upon-Tweed in 1903, aged 61. The Simpson family do not appear to have offered a home to Maria. Maria is recorded as having had previous employment, although, being listed as an '*Idiot from Childhood*' suggests lifelong intellectual difficulties.

Jane Heslop

Jane Heslop was born in Berwick-upon-Tweed. Her exact date of birth is unknown, however, in the 1841 Census she is recorded as being seven years old. She lives with her family in Walkergate Lane, Berwick-upon-Tweed. Her father, Thomas (45), is a *'Tailor,'* and her mother is called Grace (40). She has six siblings: twin brothers Christian (15), who has no occupation, and Joseph (15), who is a *'Tailor's Apprentice,'* Elizabeth (12), Matthew (10), Isabella (5), and Grace (2). In 1845, Jane's mother dies, aged 44.

Six years after her mother's death, the 1851 Census records Jane as still living with her family in Walkergate Lane. Jane is now 17, unmarried, and is listed as having the occupation of *'House Servant.'* Her father is still occupied as a *'Tailor,'* as is her unmarried brother, Matthew. Her sister, Isabella, is a *'House Servant.'* Jane is still living in Walkergate Lane and working as a *'House Servant'* in 1861. Her father is a *'Tailor and Property Agent.'* Also living in the house is James Windham (17), a *'Carpenter'*, who is Thomas Heslop's grandson.

On the 31st March, 1865, Jane, now 30, is admitted to the Northumberland County Lunatic Asylum. Records list her as being single and as having had a former occupation as a *'Domestic Servant.'* Her home address is recorded as Walkergate Lane, Berwick-upon-Tweed, and her family contact is her father, Thomas. Her *'Form of Mental Disease'* is listed as being *'Mania'* with the cause being *'Unknown.'* Her condition is described as having only occurred for the previous three months. In 1868, Jane's father dies, aged 73.

Six years after her admission, the 1871 Census records Jane as still being a patient in the County Lunatic Asylum. At this time, she is categorised as a *'Lunatic.'* Despite her condition being recorded as *'Not improved,'* Jane is discharged from the County Lunatic Asylum on the 23rd January, 1873. It is unclear whether she was discharged directly to the Berwick-upon-Tweed Union Workhouse, however, the 1881 Census records her as an Inmate there. She is unmarried and categorised as an '*Imbecile.*' Jane dies in the Workhouse on the 27th September, 1881, aged 46.

Jane lived with her family for the early part of her life. She stayed at home while her siblings left to move on with their lives and it is likely that she had a role looking after her father after he was widowed. Jane is admitted to the County Lunatic Asylum when her father was aged 70 and it may be that he was too infirm to provide her with the support she needed at that time. Her father was listed as being a '*Property Agent,*' suggesting he would have had some resources to his name, however, being a woman and a '*Lunatic,*' Jane would probably have been unable to inherit anything directly after his death.

Jane is categorised as a '*Lunatic*' when in the County Lunatic Asylum but is later categorised as an '*Imbecile*' when she returns to Berwick-upon-Tweed to live in the Workhouse. It may also be that Jane's initial admission to the County Lunatic Asylum was caused by an acute episode of mental illness and that, as the staff there grew to know her, Jane's life-long intellectual limitations may have become more apparent. This may explain why she was discharged, despite being '*Not improved*' and subsequently categorised as an '*Imbecile*' on entering the Workhouse.

Mary A Kerry

Very little verifiable information was available about the life of Mary A Kerry. Her place of birth is not known, but she is recorded as being born in 1806. In the 1881 Census she is recorded as being an Inmate of the Berwick-upon-Tweed Union Workhouse. At that time, Mary (75) is unmarried and is not listed as having any previous occupation. She is categorised as an *'Imbecile.'*

Patrick Lovell

Patrick Lovell was born in Ireland in 1815. At the age of 45, the 1861 Census records him as a married *'Labourer'* living in Cornhill, a village in a rural area to the south side of the River Tweed, near Coldstream. He lived with his wife, Barbara (37), who was also Irish, and their three children: Ann (10), Patrick (5), and Sarah (1). The children were all born in Northumberland. It is unclear what happened to Patrick and his family in the intervening years, but in the 1881 Census he is recorded as being an Inmate of the Berwick-upon-Tweed Union Workhouse. At that time, he is 66, married, and his occupation is listed as being a *'Labourer.'* Patrick is categorised as being an *'Imbecile.'* His wife is recorded in the 1881 Census as living at Newbigging Farm, Cornhill, with her daughters, Sarah and Margaret, both of whom are unmarried *'Farm Labourers.'* Also, in the house is a grandchild, Mary Carrigan (7), who is a *'Scholar.'* Patrick dies in the Workhouse on the 25th September, 1881, aged 66.

Patrick seems to have been able to work, sustain a marriage and a family for a large proportion of his life. He appears to have entered the Workhouse later in life, while the rest of his family stay together to support each other. The reason for his admission is unknown, but the fact that he dies soon after the 1881 Census record was taken may suggest that he was suffering from a debilitating terminal illness. The use of the term *'Imbecile'* in his categorisation may suggest that, whatever his condition, it may have also included cognitive decline. He would have been unlikely to meet the criteria for intellectual disability, as defined today.

Isabella Mace

Isabella Mace was born in Berwick-upon-Tweed in 1836, although in 1841, when aged five years old, she is recorded as living with her family at Queen's Court, Deptford, Greenwich. The family consisted of her father, James (40), a *'Pattern Maker,'* her mother, Elizabeth (40), and her siblings: Charles (16), John (14), Elizabeth (12), James (10), Mary (7), Andrew (3), and Margaret (1). Queen's Court no longer exists, but at the time this area was known for its slum housing.

In the 1851 Census, Isabella is still in Greenwich, but is now recorded as living with her aunt's family at 7 Charlotte Street. At the address are her aunt, Ann Smith (46), who is the sister of Isabella's father, and uncle, Joseph Smith (46), who was an *'Engineer.'* The couple also had three children of their own living with them: Joseph (14), Mary (3), and Charles (1), as well as William Smith (22), a relative with an occupation listed as a *'Wheelwright.'* At that time Isabella had no listed occupation.

At some point between 1851 and 1857, Isabella is admitted to the Royal Edinburgh Lunatic Asylum. The Minutes of the Board of Guardians of Berwick-upon-Tweed Union Workhouse note on 4th May, 1857, that payment was authorised for her to be transferred there and on 15th June, 1857, payment was ordered for Messrs Grant and Wallace for medical attendance in procuring the admission of Isabella Mace, *'a pauper lunatic,'* to the Royal Edinburgh Asylum. She was conveyed there by a George Turner, who receives payment for this from the Board of Guardians of the Workhouse on the 13th December, 1858.

She was visited on behalf of the Board of Guardians of the Workhouse by a Dr Kirkwood. His report is discussed in the Minutes of the 21st September, 1857. He recommends that Isabella remains in the Royal Edinburgh Lunatic Asylum despite her father's wishes to remove her. Over a year later, on the 13th December, 1858, payment to Dr Fluker for a Certificate of Lunacy for Isabella Mace is recorded in the Minutes. Dr Kirkwood appears to visit Isabella on a yearly basis and charts her positive progress. His report, noted in the Minutes, dated the 5th August, 1859, states that: *'Isabella Mace was much improved'* and on the 20th August, 1860: *'Isabella Mace continues to improve.'*

Shortly after this, on the 8th October, 1860, Isabella, who is now 25, is transferred from the Royal Edinburgh Lunatic Asylum to the Northumberland County Lunatic Asylum. Her admission record contains no information in the section titled *'Name and address of Relatives or Friends'* and her previous occupation is listed as being a *'Domestic Servant.'* Her *'Form of Mental Disease'* is listed as being *'Mania'* and is recorded as having been present for the previous two years.

In 1861, Isabella appears in a *'True List of all Lunatics, Idiots, and other persons of Unsound Mind, chargeable to the Common Fund or to the Parishes comprised within the Berwick-upon-Tweed Union.'* On this list she is categorised as a *'Lunatic.'* The 1861 Census also records her as being a patient of the County Lunatic Asylum. She is unmarried and categorised as being a *'Lunatic.'* On the 14th September, 1863, the Minutes of the Board of Guardians of Berwick-upon-Tweed Union record the conclusion of a report on the status of Isabella, following a visit to the County Lunatic Asylum: *'Her speedy recovery can be expected.'* This was followed by a letter, dated 2nd February, 1864, from the Berwick-upon-Tweed Union to the Clerk of the County Lunatic Asylum. This asked: *'for the permission of the Visiting Committee to remove Isabella Mace* [and another patient] *either to the Workhouse or to the custody of friends, since they are much improved in mind and health.'*

Despite this, she is still a patient in the County Lunatic Asylum ten years later in 1871, with no change in her marital status, previous occupation, or categorisation. Isabella is finally discharged from the County Lunatic Asylum on the 3rd November, 1871, her condition being *'Relieved.'*

In 1881, Isabella is back in Berwick-upon-Tweed and is living as an Inmate in the Berwick-upon-Tweed Union Workhouse. She is recorded as being single but is now categorised as being an *'Imbecile.'* She appears in the 1891 and 1901 Censuses, again as an Inmate of the Workhouse and is still categorised as an *'Imbecile.'* Isabella dies in the Workhouse on the 3rd October, 1902, aged 66.

Isabella seems to have spent the majority of her adult life in some form of institutional care. Although she was born in Berwick-upon-Tweed, her family move to Greenwich when she is still a small child. It is likely that her father moved for reasons to do with work and to obtain support from his extended family. The Census indicates that there were also a number of other people called Mace from Berwick-upon-Tweed living in the London area at the time. The area the family moved to was one of slum housing, so the move is unlikely to have created better living conditions than they might have previously experienced in Berwick-upon-Tweed.

Isabella was living with her aunt in Greenwich when she was fifteen. Although it is not recorded in the Census, we might assume that she worked for her aunt carrying out general domestic duties for her and that later references to her having been a *'Domestic Servant'* might be referring to this time. Living with a family member may have also offered her some protective status if she was not entirely capable in carrying out her duties.

It is recorded that Isabella had a period of mental illness in early adulthood. She may also have simply found it difficult to cope with the demands of adult life due to a limited intellectual capacity. She may have initially been admitted to an institution in the London area, but it was custom at the time to return paupers to the Parishes to which they belonged. Isabella was a patient of the Royal Edinburgh Lunatic Asylum prior to being transferred to the Northumberland County Lunatic Asylum, once this was opened. It was usual for paupers from Berwick-upon-Tweed to go to the Lunatic Asylum in Edinburgh, as this was the nearest large Asylum, prior to one being built in Northumberland. Her condition at the time must have warranted being placed in a Lunatic Asylum rather than the Berwick-upon-Tweed Union Workhouse. She is categorised in both the 1861 and 1871 Censuses as being as a '*Lunatic.*'

On being transferred to the Workhouse, however, she is re-categorised as an '*Imbecile.*' This might have represented an acknowledgement of her difficulties as being life-long and more related to a fundamental lack of capacity to cope independently than mental illness. Isabella remained an Inmate of the Workhouse under the category of '*Imbecile*' up until her death many years later.

Elizabeth McNab

Elizabeth McNab was born in Berwick-upon-Tweed in 1839. In the 1841 Census, she is recorded as living in Berwick-upon-Tweed, with her father, John (25), a *'Nail Maker,'* her mother, Mary (25), and younger brother, Alexander (7 months). Ten years later Elizabeth, now 13, is living in Castlegate, Berwick-upon-Tweed, with her father, mother, and three siblings: John (8), Robina (5), and James (3). In the 1861 Census, the family remain in Castlegate, with the addition of three new siblings: Mary (9), George (6), and Jennet (2). Elizabeth is not recorded as living with the family at that time. At some point, however, prior to early 1865, she was an Inmate of the Berwick-upon-Tweed Union Workhouse, as she was admitted to the Northumberland County Lunatic Asylum on the 31st March, 1865, aged 26, with the Workhouse being listed as her *'Place of Previous Abode.'* She is single and her family contact is her father, John McNab, a *'Railway Labourer.'* Her *'Form of Mental Disease'* is listed as being *'Dementia'* with the cause being *'Epilepsy.'* This is recorded as having had a duration of ten days.

The 1871 Census records Elizabeth as still being a patient in the County Lunatic Asylum. She is listed as being a *'Mason's Labourer's Daughter'* and she is categorised as being a *'Lunatic.'* Elizabeth is discharged from the County Lunatic asylum on the 22nd February, 1872, despite her condition being described as *'Not Improved.'*

In 1881, Elizabeth is back as an Inmate in the Workhouse. She is not listed as having any previous occupation and is now categorised as an *'Imbecile.'* Ten years later, aged 51, she remains in the Workhouse. She is single and is listed as having had a previous occupation as a *'General Servant.'* She remains categorised as an *'Imbecile.'*

Elizabeth is readmitted to the Northumberland County Lunatic Asylum on the 8th June, 1893, aged 54. In the section of her notes titled *'Name and Address of Relatives or Friends'* it says *'None – All Dead,'* although her mother is alive at the time and dies three years after Elizabeth's admission, aged 79. Elizabeth's *'Form of Mental Disease'* is listed as being 'Dementia with Epilepsy,' with the cause being 'Epilepsy,' and the duration being 28 years.

There is little recorded of note in the records about Elizabeth's stay in the County Lunatic Asylum, however, it is noted between the 25th February and the 24th April, 1897, that she is bed-ridden due to: '*an old ulcer on the left leg broken down, the discharge is very offensive.*' She is reported as being in good physical health in May that same year, with the notes of the 11th May, 1897, giving some insight into her mental ability:

> '*She labours under dementia with epilepsy. She cannot tell how long she has been here; she doesn't know the day, month or year. She is quite childish and unfit for rational conversation. Bodily condition – is feeble epileptic. Bodily clean, fairly well nourished and believed to be free from injury. Heart and lungs normal. Appetite good. Pulse 100, Resp. 26, Temp. 96.4°.*'

The notes generally refer to Elizabeth by her condition, rather than as a person. There is also a focus on her inability to work, although Elizabeth seems to perceive that she is helping to care for others in the Infirmary:

> 2nd October, 1897 – '*This epileptic is in the Infirmary. She imagines she looks after everybody. She is unable to do any work.*'

> 11th January, 1898 – '*This epileptic is quite stupid and sits quietly in her chair all day. She is quite untidy and general health fair.*'

Her rapid decline is charted in the notes and there is a change from referring to her as an '*epileptic*' to her briefly being described as a person, even although this is in terms of her being an '*old lady*':

> 27th April, 1898 – '*This epileptic sits as usual in her chair all day. She is going downhill very quickly.*'

4th May, 1898 – *'This old lady is in bed today owing to the fact that this morning the following: condition of her right leg and foot was noticed. The shin from just below the knee downwards is red and glossy and just below the knee is a group of pustules, each pustule about the size of a pin's head at the back and sides of the ankle – the epidermis is broken, leaving a red surface which secretes a yellowish, white fluid.'*

As her decline continues, she is referred to as a patient:

8th May, 1898 – *'Today patient seems very ill, she complains at much pain all over her body and especially pain in the chest. She has a temperature of 101.4°, her face is flushed, and she is very restless. She was examined but owing to the fact that she was muttering and talking all the time nothing definite could be made out. The breath sounds were accompanied by noise in the trachea which makes other sounds.'*

Elizabeth dies in the County Lunatic Asylum on the 8th May, 1898, at 7.20pm, aged 59. She was attended at the time of her death by a Nurse Armstrong:

9th May, 1898 – *'Patient died yesterday at 7.20pm. A post-mortem examination was made and the whole of the lower lobe of the left lung was consolidated completely. The upper lobe showed signs of hyperaemia* [NB: an excess of blood in the vessels supplying an organ or other part of the body] *but was not consolidated. In the lower lobe of the right lung was a mass about as large as a pigeon's egg, apparently a tuberculous nodule in the stage of acute softening.'*

Her *'Statement of Death'* notes the *'Apparent Cause of Death'* as *'Epileptic Marasmus'* and *'Congestion of Lung,'* the former having a duration of *'Many years'* and the latter for *'A few days.'* A post-mortem was carried out and it was noted that there were *'No unusual circumstances, no injuries'* surrounding her death and that she was not mechanically restrained.

Elizabeth appears to have had difficulties from a relatively young age and is admitted to the County Lunatic Asylum from the Workhouse. Epilepsy is the identified cause of her difficulties and she is initially considered to be suffering from *'Dementia'* as a result. She is discharged from the County Lunatic Asylum with her condition being described as *'Not Improved.'* Elizabeth then re-enters the Workhouse and becomes re-categorised as an *'Imbecile.'* Elizabeth is re-admitted to the County Lunatic Asylum later in life, where she spends her remaining years. As effective treatments for epilepsy were not properly developed until the twentieth century, it is likely that her untreated epilepsy may have led to a significantly reduced ability to function and decline in her cognitive abilities over time.

Elizabeth Morgan

Elizabeth Morgan was born in Tweedmouth in 1850. The following year she is recorded as living with her family in Kiln Hill, Tweedmouth, under her maiden name, Davidson. Her mother, Catherine Davidson (35), is head of the household, married, and a 'Lodging House Keeper.' Also living at home are her siblings: Francis (17), unmarried and a 'Rope Maker,' James (13), also a 'Rope Maker,' and Oswald (7), a 'Scholar' at the 'Ragged School.'

In the 1861 Census, Elizabeth is again recorded as living at home with her family in Kiln Hill. She is now a 'Scholar.' The household comprises of: her mother (46), who is widowed, her brother, James (23), who is married to Ann (24), and a 'Labourer,' and their child James, (3 months), and her brother Oswald, who is now a 'Labourer.' Marcy Flannigan, who is 14 years old, is recorded as being a visitor at this time.

Ten years later, the household at Kiln Hill has reduced to Elizabeth and her mother. Her mother is now a 'Pensioner' and Elizabeth is a 'General Domestic Servant.' Elizabeth marries James Morgan in 1871. In the 1881 Census, aged 31, she is recorded as living in the Berwick-upon-Tweed Union Workhouse. She is listed as being married, but without any previous occupation. She is categorised as an 'Imbecile.' In the same year, the Census indicates Elizabeth's mother is still living at 42 Kiln Hill, as the head of the household, with Elizabeth's husband James, who is a 'General Labourer,' and their daughter, Margaret, who is aged four.

Elizabeth is admitted to the Northumberland County Lunatic Asylum on the 25th January, 1884, aged 36. She is listed as being the 'Wife of James Morgan, General Labourer' and his home address is 7 Weatherly Square, Berwick-upon-Tweed. Elizabeth's 'Place of Former Abode,' however, is listed as being 46 West End, Tweedmouth, suggesting that the couple were living apart. Her 'Form of Mental Disease' is listed as being 'Melancholia' (depression) with the cause being 'Unknown.' Her condition is recorded as having lasted for the previous 18 years and as having begun when she was only fifteen years old.

Elizabeth remains in the County Lunatic Asylum up until her death on the 28th February, 1899, aged 48. During that time, there is only very limited information available about her life. On the 1st September, 1896, it was noted that there was *'No change in this demented woman. Works in the kitchen. Health good.'* Four months later she appeared to have deteriorated, with the notes of the 31st December, 1896, recording that:

'She can understand little about her work, understanding simple questions; memory for recent and remote events is bad…she often talks to herself.'

While no official record was found of Elizabeth having had more than one child, on the 20th September, 1897, it is noted that she had the *'Delusion that she can hear her children crying sometimes.'*

A period of physical ill health followed. On the 15th December, 1897, the notes report that she is in the Infirmary with a *'discharging wound'* until the 29th March, 1898. Her abscess returns on the 18th July, 1898, and she was in the Infirmary on the 27th October, 1898. On the 10th January, 1899, she is reported as: *'weak and gradually fading,'* and on the 28th February, 1899, that: *'She lay gasping for breath and died today at 12 noon.'*

Her *'Statement of Death'* records her apparent cause of death as *'Phthisis Pulmonalis'* (Tuberculosis). No post-mortem was carried out, there were *'no unusual circumstances,' 'no injuries'* surrounding her death, and she did not undergo mechanical restraint. The duration of her illness was said to be *'Many months.'* The name of the person who was with her at her death was Nurse Kelly.

Elizabeth was 48 when she died. It is of note that Elizabeth continued to live with her mother while her siblings moved on elsewhere. She had a different address to her husband at the time of her admission to the

County Lunatic Asylum, perhaps suggesting that the relationship was not a supportive one. Elizabeth's difficulties are noted as beginning in her teenage years and appear to be depressive in nature. She was not categorised as being an *'Imbecile'* whilst in the County Lunatic Asylum and this may suggest that her difficulties stemmed primarily from long-standing mental health problems. The County Lunatic Asylum notes do, however, refer to her as being *'demented'* and as having poor memory. Her limited understanding about her work and her difficulty in answering simple questions, suggests that she may also have had an intellectual disability.

Charles Pringle

Charles Pringle was born in 1821 in Woolwich, Kent. In the 1861 Census, he is recorded as living in Church Street Soup Kitchen Yard, Berwick-upon-Tweed. He is 36, unmarried, and his occupation is listed as a *'Labourer.'* In the 1881 Census, Charles, is recorded as being aged 60 and as being an Inmate in the Berwick-upon-Tweed Union Workhouse. He is listed as being unmarried and as having no previous occupation. He is categorised as an *'Imbecile.'*

Charles is admitted to the Northumberland County Lunatic Asylum from the Workhouse on the 16th May, 1888, with his age being noted as 65. His *'Condition of Life and Previous Occupation'* is listed as a *'General Labourer'* and in the *'Name and Address of Relatives or Friends'* section is recorded *'None, No Friends.'* His *'Place of Previous Abode'* was the Workhouse and his *'Form of Mental Disease'* is listed as *'Dementia.'* Charles was still a patient in the County Lunatic Asylum in 1891.

Some information is available about his later life in the County Lunatic Asylum. On the 25th September, 1895, it is recorded that:

'This man works with the garden party is of only very little use. Quite demented and never speaks to anyone. Has good bodily health.'

On the 11th December, 1895, he suffered a shoulder injury. It is noted that:

'This patient continues to work outside as usual until today when he was brought in fallen forward on to his shoulder whilst squatting to defecate in the grounds.'

The notes document him receiving care for his shoulder injury, which appears to have healed by the 20th January, 1896. He appears to be viewed as a sullen, quiet man, with generally good physical health, but as having a chronic, unchanging condition in respect of his mental health. The notes on the 22nd January, 1896, state that he was: *'mentally unchanged: a chronic dementia,'* on the 25th December, 1896: *'No change. Works with garden party. Silent and taciturn. Health fair,'* and on the 5th April, 1897: *'No change mentally. Still continuing in garden. Only speaks when spoken to. Health good. 118lbs.'*

A period of poor physical health follows shortly afterwards. Charles is admitted to the Infirmary with a cough (bronchitis) on the 27th April, 1897. He remains there until the 3rd May, 1897, when it is reported that *'He is up and about again.'* Later that year he suffers from oedema and is frequently bedridden:

12th July, 1897 – *'Quite idle. In and out of bed on account of oedema in legs and feet. No overall change.'*

This takes a while to resolve and on the 29th September, 1897, it is reported that Charles is:

'Now unable to do any work. Suffers from oedema of foot and of a hernia. No change at all. Health good. 119lbs.'

He becomes bed-ridden on the 29th October, 1897, due to his oedema: *'Is now in bed.'* There is some improvement in November and on the 22nd November, 1897, it is noted that: *'This man will probably be able to get up shortly.'* Unfortunately, however, Charles then suffers from a stroke:

6th December, 1897 – *'This morning about 7.20 am, this old man was seized with a stroke which appeared to be due to a small haemorrhage.'*

While still in bed on the 12th December, 1897, it was noted that: *'This P. appears now to have completely recovered from his stroke.'* A week later Charles was *'Now up and out of bed,'* although he was still weak and unable to resume his work for some time:

13th January, 1898 – *'Has been out of the Infirmary about a fortnight. Is too feeble to do any work. Very quiet and habits clean.'*

On the 3rd March, 1898, the notes indicate that he is in bed again due to his oedema. He is transferred to the Infirmary again and he stays there until the 29th September. On the 14th November, 1898, the notes indicate that he is still in poor health. There appears to be little consideration of the impact this might have on him and there is instead a focus on his manner and bad language: *'He is surly and addicted to bad language as ever'* and:

21st November, 1898 – *'He remains in poor health. He is surly and uses very bad language.'*

1st December, 1898 – *'He is very noisy day and night – frequently getting out of bed and is constantly swearing.'*

On the 28th December, 1898, the notes indicate that he is weakening and on the 25th January, 1899: *'He is getting to look rather thin and frail.'* A gradual deterioration and an increased dependency are noted. On the 25th March, 1899, it is reported that Charles *'Is now unable to get out of bed without assistance.'* There remains a focus on his behaviour and on the 29th March, 1899, the notes indicate that he continues to swear and be abusive to others. The staff report that it was hard to examine him and there was a *'constant chatter of abuse.'* On the 30th March, 1899, it is recorded that: *'He died at 11pm last night.'* Charles died on the 29th March, 1899. He was aged 76 and single at the time of his death. His *'Statement of Death'* recorded his cause of death as *'Phthisis Pulmonalis'* (Tuberculosis). A post-mortem was conducted, and no unusual circumstances or injuries were noted. The duration of his disease was *'A few months.'* No mechanical restraint was used. The person present at his death was '*Attendant Dick.*'

It is interesting that Charles remained in institutions in the Northumberland area rather than being returned to the Parish where he was born. He was not married but he may have had some entitlement under the 1846 Irremovable Poor Act, allowing him to stay. Charles enters the Workhouse later in life. On his subsequent transfer to the County Lunatic Asylum, his records indicate that he had '*Dementia.*' He spends his remaining days there, until his death at age 76. Charles' difficulties appear to occur later in his life. There is no clear evidence that he had life-long significant intellectual difficulties, but this remains a possibility as his previous work was relatively unskilled.

John Richardson

John Richardson was born in 1869 in Scremerston. In the 1871 Census, John is recorded as being two years old and living with his family in Tweedmouth. John's father, also called John (40), is a *'General Labourer.'* Also in the household, are his mother, Mary Ann (37), and siblings: Alexander (16), unmarried and a *'General Labourer,'* Joseph (14), also a *'General Labourer,'* Thomas (7), a *'Scholar,'* and Mary Ann (5), also a *'Scholar.'* Also living with the family as a *'Boarder'* is Robert Rutherford (48), who is a *'Worker in a Bone Mill.'* John's father dies in 1874 and, in the 1881 Census, John is recorded as living in the Berwick-upon-Tweed Union Workhouse. He is only 12 years old and is the only child in the Workhouse categorised as an *'Imbecile.'* Five years later, on the 2nd February, 1886, John is admitted to the Northumberland County Lunatic Asylum. In the section in his case notes titled *'Condition of Life and Previous Occupation'* the word *'None'* is written. His mother is listed as his family contact and her address is recorded as Main Street, Tweedmouth. John's *'Place of Previous Abode'* is listed as being the Workhouse. His *'Form of Mental Disease'* is listed as *'Idiocy'* and the *'Supposed Cause of Insanity'* as *'Congenital.'*

In the 1891 Census, he is still resident in the County Lunatic Asylum and is categorised as an *'Imbecile from Childhood,'* with no previously listed occupation. The notes from 1895 onwards give some indication of John's behaviour and level of understanding. On the 16th October, 1895, it is recorded that:

'This idiot remains unchanged. He runs purposelessly about the airing court: grins and gesticulates. Is clean and tidy in dress. In good general health. Does nothing.'

Nearly a year later, on the 7th September, 1896, the picture of John as a healthy, excitable, noisy man, with limited skills and understanding, remains consistent:

'This lad can't say an intelligible word but can make a great deal of noise. Is in good health. Can't do much for himself but when cleaned and tidied doesn't alter things for the worse.'

On the 30th December, 1896, John is described as: '*Aphasic, grotesque, irresponsible, this idiot remains just the same. General health good. 138lbs.*' The notes hint at an expectation that John should be changing and improving, as his lack of progress is consistently noted. On the 12th July, 1897, he is described as: '*Quite stupid. No change of any kind.*' His inability to work or earn money is also noted on a few occasions. On the 29th September, 1897, he is noted as being: '*Quite unable to do anything, earn or speak;*' on the 15th January, 1898, it is reported that: '*He does not work. At times he becomes excitable;*' while on 29th January, 1899, the staff write: '*Can't get anything out of him. Does no work. Can feed himself and takes his food well.*' There is some indication that his lack of contribution may be due to laziness, rather than inability, as on the 9th July, 1902, it is noted: '*He is inclined to be idle but not vicious.*'

There are a series of entries reporting '*no change*' in John throughout 1898 to 1901, with only the occasional reference to more than this. These entries build a picture of an energetic, excitable man who likes to have the attention of others. On the 19th April, 1898, it is reported: '*He is very childish in manner, at times excited.*' On the 7th July, 1899, the notes state: '*Still as much like a monkey as ever.*' Unusually, there is also an indication that John is viewed fondly, at least by some staff members, with the notes referring to him by the nickname '*Jacko.*' On 18th January, 1901, his notes state: '*Jacko is quite unchanged. Likes to be taken notice of.*' Other staff were much more impersonal, referring to him by his categorisation of '*Idiot.*' On the 27th April, 1901, his notes state: '*There is no change in this idiot. He continues with his grotesque antics.*'

Between 1902 and 1912, the entries record '*no change*' in John in a variety of ways. On the 20th September, 1912, the final entry simply states: '*Transferred to Huddersfield Asylum.*'

As indicated in the County Lunatic Asylum notes and confirmed in both the 1901 and 1911 Censuses, John's place of residence is unchanged until 1912, and he is categorised as an *'Idiot'* in both Censuses. John is transferred to the West Riding County Asylum (also known as Storthes Hall or Huddersfield Asylum) on the 20th September, 1912. On discharge from the Northumberland County Lunatic Asylum, he is listed as *'Not Improved.'* John dies in the West Riding County Asylum on the 9th April, 1913, aged 44.

John was only a child when he was admitted to the Workhouse following the death of his father. He is specifically mentioned in the Visiting Commissioner's report of the 16th February, 1880, and recommendations are made for him to be transferred:

'There is one boy, John Richardson, who would undoubtedly be much benefitted by being sent to some idiot institution. He is now nine years of age and the Master informs me that he has improved since he has been in the house, that being the case, he is eminently likely to be able to be taught some useful trade.'

We can clearly see the outcome of this for John. Although he remains in the Workhouse at least until the time of the 1881 Census, he is transferred to the County Lunatic Asylum when he is sixteen years old.

The reality of this transfer is that he becomes institutionalised and does not move on from a life in care. Over time, his records become more difficult to trace, his presence being recorded using only his initials, rather than his name, and his place of origin often being left blank on Census records. He appears to have had the developmental history of someone with a more severe intellectual disability and he would have been unlikely to have benefitted from living in an institution for people with mental health problems. This is reflected in the many entries in his notes that chart a lack of change over a period of many years. He is later transferred to a newly opened Asylum in Huddersfield that had specific provision for people with an intellectual disability. Unfortunately, John died soon after being transferred, at the relatively young age of 44.

Bridget Robertson

Bridget Robertson was born in Ireland in 1838. In the 1871 Census, she is recorded as living with her husband in Tweedmouth. Bridget is 26 years old and her husband is George Robertson (35), who was born in Aberdeen, Scotland. His occupation is listed as being a *'Coach Fitter.'*

In the 1881 Census, Bridget, now 43, is recorded as being an Inmate of the Berwick-upon-Tweed Union Workhouse. She is listed as being married, with no previous occupation recorded. She is categorised as an *'Imbecile.'* In 1891, Bridget is still an Inmate of the Workhouse. She is listed as having a previous occupation as a *'Field Worker.'* She is now categorised as an *'Idiot from Childhood.'* Also, in the Workhouse in 1891, is her husband, George Robertson.

Bridget is admitted to the Northumberland County Lunatic Asylum on the 3rd June, 1893, aged 55. Her *'Condition of Life and Previous Occupation'* is listed as being a *'Hawker's Wife'* and in the section in her case notes titled *'Name and Address of Relatives or Friends'* it is recorded: *'George Robertson, Husband, Hawker, Union Workhouse, Berwick-upon-Tweed.'* Her *'Place of Previous Abode'* is listed as being the *'Union Workhouse, Berwick-upon-Tweed.'* Her *'Form of Mental Disease'* is listed as *'Epilepsy,'* as is the *'Supposed Cause of Insanity.'* Her condition is recorded as having been ongoing for the last 15 years and to have started when she was 40. Bridget dies in the County Lunatic Asylum on the 29th December, 1899, aged 61. Her cause of death is recorded as being *'Epileptic Exhaustion.'*

It is difficult to speculate about Bridget's early life without information about her maiden name. She seems to have worked as a *'Field Worker'* and she later married a man who lived in impoverished circumstances. She develops epilepsy at the age of 40 and this may have exacerbated any difficulties in her capacity to cope, leading her to live in institutions for the remaining years of her life.

Thomas Robertson

Thomas Robertson was born in Berwick-upon-Tweed in 1841. In the Census of that year, he is recorded as being just one month old and living with his family in High Greens, Berwick-upon-Tweed. His father is also called Thomas Robertson (35) and his occupation is listed as an *'Agricultural Labourer.'* Also, at home, are his mother, Ann (30), and his young siblings: Alexander (10), Alison (8), and John (5). In the 1851 Census, Thomas, now a *'Scholar,'* is recorded as living with his family in Castlegate, Berwick-upon-Tweed, with his parents and brothers: Alexander, an *'Agricultural Labourer,'* John, an *'Apprentice Butcher,'* and Robert (4). Also, living in the household is James Dickson (20), who is a nephew of Thomas' parents and who is listed as being an *'Agricultural Labourer.'*

In the 1861 Census, Thomas, now 20, unmarried, and a *'Butcher,'* is recorded as still living in Castlegate, with his parents and siblings. His father is now a *'Railway Worker,'* his brother John is a *'Butcher,'* and his brother Robert is a *'Scholar.'* Also living in the household is Andrew Taylor (7), who is a grandson of Thomas' parents. In the 1881 Census, Thomas is recorded as being an Inmate of the Berwick-upon-Tweed Union Workhouse. He is 40, unmarried, and his previous occupation is listed as being a *'Butcher.'* He is categorised as an *'Imbecile.'*

Thomas is admitted to the Northumberland County Lunatic Asylum on the 28th March, 1890, aged 48. He is single and his *'Condition of Life and Previous Occupation'* is listed as being a *'Butcher, Journeyman.'* His family contact is listed as being his sister, Alice Taylor, 31 Woolmarket, Berwick-upon-Tweed, and his *'Place of Previous Abode'* is the Workhouse. His *'Form of Mental Disease'* is recorded as *'Dementia with Aphasia'* and the *'Supposed Cause of Insanity'* is *'Unknown.'* The *'Duration of Existing Attacks'* is 11½ years and the *'Age at First Attack'* is 37. Thomas is still in the County Lunatic Asylum at the time of the 1891 and 1901 Censuses. On both occasions he is categorised as a *'Lunatic.'*

Little is known about Thomas' early years in the County Lunatic Asylum. He seemed capable of work, although the notes give an impression of a frail man with a quick temper. On the 22nd January, 1898, it is noted that: *'He is employed out of doors on the farm. He is not able for heavy work. He is excitable and easily angered. Health fair, Weight 135lbs.'*

His work appears to be satisfactory and on the 22nd April, 1898, it is noted that: *'He is employed in the grounds and works well,'* although he does not initiate conversation. On the 22nd July, 1898, staff report that: *'He is silent, only speaking when spoken to.'* An impression is given of a man who is compliant, who generally works well, but who can become aggressive if prevented from engaging in his routines. On the 26th January, 1899, his notes state: *'Clean, tidy. He is noisy at times and becomes very abusive if interfered with at all. He is demented and agrees to anything one suggests to him.'* Only a few references are made in relation to his intellectual abilities. On the 24th January, 1901, it is reported that he: *'Is very stupid. Simply says "Aye and No."'*

In April 1901, it is noted that Thomas is physically unwell. On the 7th June, 1901, a mass is found in his tongue: *'The case is undoubtably one of carcinoma of tongue. It is inoperable.'* His condition deteriorates and on the 15th July, 1901, it is recorded that: *'This poor old man seems to be getting weaker every day.'* Thomas has ongoing difficulties with swallowing and eating, and on the 30th September, 1901, it is reported that: *'This patient is now in bed in the infirmary complaining of weakness.'* Thomas dies on 10th October, 1901, aged 59: *'This man became gradually weaker and he died at 6 o'clock this morning.'*

His *'Statement of Death'* notes the cause of death as *'Cancer of Tongue,'* with a duration of disease of *'about 1 year.'* No post-mortem was conducted, there was no mechanical restraint used, and the person present at death was *'Attendant Dick.'*

Thomas Robertson starts his life in a fairly ordinary way, being raised by his family and working as a butcher. He enters the Workhouse and is later transferred to the County Lunatic Asylum. As a part of the process his categorisation is changed from *'Imbecile'* to *'Lunatic.'* A deterioration in his mental state and speech are indicated by the terms *'Dementia'* and *'Aphasia.'* Thomas dies of a physical illness – cancer of the tongue.

It is not entirely clear why Thomas was categorised as an *'Imbecile'* in the Workhouse. One possible indicator of him having significant intellectual difficulties is that he is referred to as having been a *'Butcher, Journeyman.'* This might suggest that he did not hold a responsible position as a butcher but had always worked under supervision.

Dorothy Scott

Dorothy Scott was born in Spittal, in 1843. In the 1851 Census, she is seven years old and a *'Scholar.'* She is living in Tweedmouth with her father, George Scott (40), a *'Labourer,'* her mother, Jane Scott (45), and her older sister, Elizabeth (9), a *'Scholar.'* In the 1861 Census, Dorothy, who has no listed occupation, remains living with her family in Tweedmouth. Her brother, William (9), a *'Scholar,'* lives with the family, but her sister is no longer listed as staying at the family home.

Ten years later, the family has moved to Parliament Close, Tweedmouth. Dorothy is now 27 and has no recorded occupation. Her father is now a *'Moulder,'* and her mother is recorded as being blind. Her brother, William, is a *'Confectioner.'* Also, in the household is James Scott (2), who is listed as being her parent's grandson. In 1878, Dorothy's mother dies. Three years later, Dorothy is recorded as being an Inmate of the Berwick-upon-Tweed Union Workhouse, with a previous occupation of *'Field Worker.'* She is categorised as being an *'Imbecile.'* Her father, a *'Former Foundry Worker,'* and brother, William, a *'Confectioner,'* live at 4 Parliament Close. Dorothy returns to her family, with the 1891 Census recording her living at 4 Parliament Close with her brother. William is a *'Confectioner,'* while Dorothy is not listed as having any occupation.

Dorothy is admitted to the Northumberland County Lunatic Asylum on the 11th August, 1898, aged 54. She is listed as being unmarried and the word *'None'* is recorded in the section of her notes titled *'Condition of Life and Previous Occupation.'* Her brother, William, still living at 4 Parliament Close, is listed as her family contact. Her *'Place of Previous Abode'* is recorded as being the Workhouse. Her *'Form of Mental Disease'* is *'Mania/Delusional Insanity'* and the *'Supposed Cause of Insanity'* is *'Change of Life/Previous Attacks.'* The *'Duration of Existing Attacks'* is recorded as *'A few days'* and her first attack was at the age of 41. She is still living in the County Lunatic Asylum in 1901 and is categorised as being a *'Lunatic.'*

The County Lunatic Asylum notes provide some insight into Dorothy's life and how the staff perceived her during her later years in institutional care. On the 29th January, 1907, it is noted that:

'This patient is very noisy and abusive in the early morning and scolds the pictures and other furniture for 1 or 2 hours. Later in the day she is quiet and very civil. Does some rough work such as carrying a heavy tray to and from the kitchen. Smokes a great deal. Her bodily health is good. Habits clean and tidy. Weight 128lbs.'

On the 23rd June, 1907, she appears to be in good physical health: *'Patient does a little rough work. Is clean and tidy. Eats and sleeps well. Her bodily health is good,'* with little change in her condition reported throughout 1907. On the 29th October, 1907, it is reported that:

'There is no change to report in this patient's condition, mentally or physically.'

Dorothy appeared to suffer from extreme changes in mood, which today might be considered indicative of bipolar disorder. On the 21st January, 1908, it is reported that:

'This patient appears to be becoming rather stupid. Was in a stuporose condition for about 3 days. Refuses to speak or move but lay in bed with eyes shut and absolutely still. She takes her food and sleeps well. Does no work now. Health good.'

By contrast, on the 18th April, 1908, her behaviour is described as being much more animated:

'She is at times rather noisy and quarrels with other patients. Health good. Weighs 111lbs.'

This is followed by a pattern of reduced activity:

> 5th October, 1908 – *'This patient has not been so noisy of late. She is clean and tidy in her habits. Does little work. Health good.'*

> 15th January, 1909 – *'Patient continues to be quiet. She is in good health.'*

The next phase appears to begin on the 27th August, 1909, when it is reported that:

> *'Patient is being noisy and abusive in the early morning but becomes quieter during the day. Does some rough work in the kitchens. Health good. Weight 145lbs.'*

Similarly, on the 27th November, 1909:

> *'Patient remains noisy and abusive in the early morning. Sometimes quarrels with the other patients. Habits clean. Health good. Weight 155lb.'*

This fluctuating pattern was noted in her Continuation Certificate dated the 11th July, 1910:

> *'She labours under delusional insanity with occasional excitement or depression. She states that Edinburgh Castle belongs to her family and that she is related to Queen Elizabeth. Bodily condition is good. Body clean. Well-nourished and believed to be free from injury. Appetite good. Pulse 60. Temperature 97.8°.'*

She is reported to be *'unchanged mentally'* on the 19th December, 1910, and as being *'quiet, clean and tidy and a good worker,'* and as *'retaining her delusions'* on the 30th June, 1911. She appears to have been relatively stable throughout 1911, with the notes consistently recording 'No change.' Her mental state, however, appears to deteriorate in 1912:

28th June, 1912 – *'Patient secretes all kinds of rubbish on her person. Is demented. Quite incoherent and incomprehensible and incapable of rational conversation. Does a little needlework occasionally.'*

She also develops scabies that September:

'Patient has developed scabies and is under treatment in bed. In all other respects unchanged.'

Her mental health continues to deteriorate throughout 1913:

19th March, 1913 – *'Patient is demented now. So incoherent in her answers as to be quite unintelligible. Hoards all kinds of rubbish. Incapable of any work. In good health. Eats and sleeps well.'*

30th September, 1913 – *'Patient quite demented. Chatters incoherently and quite unintelligibly. Very slovenly in her dress and habits.'*

This is accompanied by poor physical health, with the notes charting her deterioration:

18th February, 1914 – *'A night or so ago patient had a sudden collapse. Became cold and clammy and almost pulseless. She was sent to bed and a hot water bottle was applied to her and stimulants given with a satisfactory result. In exam of chest, heart found very much affected. Patient has been losing weight and looking frail.'*

1st March, 1914 – *'With rest in bed patient improved. Her heart condition is feeble and she faints with the slightest exertion. Appetite now good. Habits clean.'*

14th March, 1914 – *'Patient has frequent fainting attacks over any exertion. She lies in a stuporose state without speaking or taking notice of her surroundings. Appetite poor.'*

30th March, 1914 – *'Very cyanose and pulse so feeble as to be uninterpretable. Strychnine given tonight. Appetite poor.'*

Dorothy dies in the County Lunatic Asylum on the 8th April, 1914, aged 69, with the notes simply recording: *'Died this morning.'* Her *'Statement of Death'* notes her *'Form of Mental Disease at Death'* as being *'Dementia'* and the cause of her death as *'Cardiovascular Disease,'* with a duration of *'several years.'* It is recorded that there were no unusual circumstances and no injuries in relation to her death, and no restraint was used. The person present at her death was *'Nurse A Balmer.'*

Dorothy lives with her family for much of her life. Following her mother's death and with her father aging, she enters the Workhouse. She does, however, leave the Workhouse and returns home to live with her brother. This is not sustained. She is later admitted to the County Lunatic Asylum, with records indicating a deteriorating mental state. She lives out her remaining days there, eventually dying of cardiovascular disease. It is unclear whether Dorothy had a history of significant intellectual difficulties, however, her County Lunatic Asylum notes give clear indications of mental health issues.

Philip Spence

Philip Spence was born in Tweedmouth in 1843. In the 1851 Census, Philip is listed as being seven years old and a *'Scholar.'* He is living with his family in Tweedmouth, which comprises his widowed mother, Margaret Spence (55), who is listed as having previously been a *'Servant,'* his sister, Mary (22), unmarried and a *'Dressmaker,'* and his brother, Richard (14), a *'Tailor'*.

In the 1861 Census, Philip (17), is recorded as living with the Grahame family in Western Lane, Berwick-upon-Tweed. He is unmarried and working as a *'Baker'* for Thomas Grahame, who is also a *'Baker.'* Ten years later, Philip is living at Bridge End, Tweedmouth with his sister, Mary, who is unmarried and a *'Dressmaker,'* and his nephew, William (13). Philip remains unmarried and his occupation is listed as being an *'Engine Cleaner.'* In 1881, Philip is recorded as being an Inmate of the Berwick-upon-Tweed Union Workhouse. His previous occupation is recorded as being a *'Baker'* and he is categorised as an *'Imbecile.'* His sister, Mary, continues to live in Tweedmouth with her son.

On 6th March, 1883, it is recorded that there is a letter to a Dr Fraser, of Ravensdowne, from Philip Spence *'desiring his discharge.'* It is requested that: *'If Dr Fraser thinks him fit to be discharged could he inform the Master of the Workhouse accordingly.'*

In the 1891 Census, Philip (48), is recorded as being an Inmate of the South Shields Union Workhouse, Harton Colliery, Harton, Durham. He is listed as being unmarried and as having had a previous occupation as a *'Baker, Journeyman.'* He is not listed as having any disability when in the Workhouse. Philip dies in the South Shields Union Workhouse in 1898, aged 56.

Philip was born when his mother was 48 years old and his father died when he was just a small child. He initially leaves home to work as a baker, but later returns to live with his sister, Mary, and her son. He enters the Berwick-upon-Tweed Union Workhouse in his thirties, where he is categorised as an '*Imbecile*.' He is subsequently recorded as living in the South Shields Union Workhouse where he eventually ends his days. This might suggest he left the Workhouse in Berwick to take up employment in the South Shields area. When this failed, he would have entered the Workhouse in South Shields. That he remained there, rather than being returned to the Workhouse in Berwick, suggests that there may have been some connection with the South Shields area that justified him staying there. It is also of note that he was no longer categorised as an '*Imbecile*' while in the South Shields Union Workhouse, suggesting that his intellectual impairment, if any, was likely to have been mild.

Margaret Todd

Margaret Todd was born in Berwick-upon-Tweed in 1832. In the 1841 Census, aged nine, she is recorded as living with her family in Upper Ravensdowne, Berwick-upon-Tweed. Her mother, Isabella, and father, William, are both 45 and the latter is a '*Mariner.*' Also at this address are her siblings: George (20), William (16), Robert (15), Mary (7), and Martin (3). The three eldest boys are all listed as '*Apprentices.*' Ten years later, Margaret is still living in Ravensdowne, with her parents and her brother, Martin. Margaret is now a '*Teacher.*' The family also have a lodger, Elizabeth Laura, who is 84. In the 1861 Census, only Margaret and her parents are living in Ravensdowne. She is listed as being a '*Teacher in a School,*' while her father, who is now 68, is listed as a '*Late Mariner.*' The living situation is unchanged in 1871, although Margaret, still unmarried, is now a '*Housekeeper.*' In 1873, both of Margaret's parents die.

In the 1881 Census, Margaret is recorded as being an Inmate of the Berwick-upon-Tweed Union Workhouse. She is listed as being unmarried, with a previous occupation of '*Schoolmistress.*' She is categorised as an '*Imbecile.*' Margaret dies in the Workhouse on the 22nd December, 1884, aged 52.

Margaret lived with her parents until their death. She worked for a consistent period of time as a schoolteacher, which would indicate that she did not have significant intellectual difficulties, although she did not leave home as her other siblings did, perhaps suggesting a need for family support. Her occupation changes from teacher to housekeeper. She could have had problems sustaining her job as a teacher, or the change may have occurred to simply allow her to look after her aging parents. Margaret enters the Workhouse sometime after her parents' deaths. She is then categorised as an '*Imbecile.*' It is unclear why she was categorised in this way. She may have led a protected existence up until that point and struggled to cope on her own, without the support of her parents.

Elizabeth Trainer

Elizabeth Trainer was born in New York, America, in 1831. Her future husband, Ralph Trainer, at the time of the 1851 Census was living in Walkergate Lane, Berwick-upon-Tweed. He was aged 39 at that time, widowed, and a *'Bootmaker.'* It is unclear how the couple met, but, at some point before 1865, Elizabeth came to England.

She was admitted to the Northumberland County Lunatic Asylum on the 20th December, 1865. The records list her as being 33, married, and a *'Shoemaker's Wife.'* Ralph Trainer, her husband, who was then living in Church Street, Berwick-upon-Tweed, was listed as her family contact. In 1870, Elizabeth's husband dies, aged 55. A year later, Elizabeth was still a patient in the County Lunatic Asylum. She is listed as having had a previous occupation of *'House Duties.'* She is categorised as being a *'Lunatic.'* She is discharged the following year, on the 22nd February, 1872. It is unclear where she was discharged to, but she still had relatives by marriage living in Berwick-upon-Tweed and she may have returned there. In 1874, her brother-in-law, John Trainer dies, aged 67.

In the 1881 Census, aged 50, she is recorded as being an Inmate in the Berwick-upon-Tweed Union Workhouse. She is recorded as being married, although her husband had died in 1870, and has no previous occupation listed. At that time, she is categorised as being an *'Imbecile.'* Her sister-in-law, Catherine Trainer (72), is also recorded as being in the Workhouse at that time, suggesting that the family may have become impoverished following the death of John Trainer. Catherine dies shortly after, aged 73.

Elizabeth is re-admitted to the County Lunatic Asylum on the 3rd December, 1886. She is now *'Widowed'* and her *'Condition of Life and Previous Occupation'* is recorded as *'Been in Workhouse for 14 years.'* Her daughter, Elizabeth Trainer, who is listed as residing with Mrs Guthrie in Main Street, Spittal, is recorded as her family contact. Her *'Place of Previous Abode'* is noted as being the Workhouse. Her *'Form of Mental Disease'* is recorded as being *'Dementia'* and the *'Supposed Cause of*

Insanity' as '*Unknown.*' The '*Duration of Existing Attacks*' is recorded as '*Been getting worse for 6 months*' and her first attack is noted as occurring at the age of 34.

In 1891, she remains a patient in the County Lunatic Asylum. Despite being widowed, she is recorded as being married and as having had a previous occupation of '*House Duties.*' She is categorised as a '*Lunatic.*' Very little is recorded about her time in the County Lunatic Asylum, with only brief hints as to what her life was like:

19th November, 1894 – '*A chronic demented. Sits for the whole day doing nothing. Saying little and thinking little. Bodily health poor and is subject to a chronic eczema on the neck. Weight 90lbs.*'

Her physical decline is documented, beginning on the 1st January, 1895, when the notes indicate her to be in the Infirmary with '*Chronic oedema of the feet.*' Her decline continues, and on the 20th January, 1895, it is reported that she is '*Still in bed and losing strength. Has occasional diarrhoea. Not taking her food.*' Her decline is very rapid:

31st January, 1895 – '*Still continues to lose strength and is now very prostrate. Mentally quite demented. Will not reply to questions.*'

8th February, 1895 – '*She has become severely purged; gradually becoming weaker and weaker. Mentally quite unchanged.*'

15th February, 1895 – '*She is now in an extremely feeble state of health and is daily losing strength. Mentally unchanged.*'

Elizabeth dies in the County Lunatic Asylum on the 18th February, 1895, aged 63. The notes record that: '*She passed away at 2.53am yesterday.*' Her '*Statement of Death*' gives her cause of death as '*General Tuberculosis,*' with a duration of '*several months.*' She died in the presence of '*Nurse Murray.*'

Elizabeth's history is somewhat unusual. She is recorded as having been born in New York, America, but becomes the wife of Ralph Trainer, a shoemaker from Berwick-upon-Tweed. It may be that Ralph went to America, as many people did during that period, to try to make his fortune, and met Elizabeth while there. His return to Berwick-upon-Tweed with his new wife could have been for a number of reasons. He may have been unsuccessful in his endeavours or they may have returned because of the American Civil War and the riots that occurred in New York around this time in response to drafting.

Elizabeth appears to have had long-standing difficulties and spent a significant part of her life in the County Lunatic Asylum, both before and after her husband's death. There is little to indicate why she was categorised as an '*Imbecile*' when in the Workhouse, as her main difficulties appear to relate to her poor mental health.

Margaret Turnbull

Margaret Turnbull was born in 1830 in New Heaton, Cornhill. In the 1851 Census, aged 21, she is recorded as living with her family in Twizel, a rural area of Northumberland. At home are her father, William (52), her mother, Ellen (50), and her siblings: Thomas (17), John (15), and William (12). Margaret's father dies in 1854, aged 54.

Ten years later, Margaret is still living in Twizel, with her two daughters, Ellen (5), and Elizabeth (2), and her mother. In 1862, however, Margaret, who is now 32, appears on a *'List of Lunatics, Idiots and other persons of Unsound Mind, Chargeable to the Common Fund or Parishes within the Berwick-upon-Tweed Union.'* Her mother is listed as living *'at Tiptoe.'* Margaret's mother dies in 1866, aged 65.

In the 1871 Census, Margaret is recorded as living as a boarder with her uncle, William Hogg (66), aunt, Mary Ann Hogg (65), and their family in a Public House in Duddo, Northumberland. Her daughters Ellen and Elizabeth are with her. Also living in the household is Margaret's cousin, Elizabeth Hogg (28).

In 1881 Margaret (51), is recorded as being an Inmate of the Berwick-upon-Tweed Union Workhouse. She is unmarried and her previous occupation is listed as being a *'Field Worker.'* She is categorised as being an *'Imbecile.'* Her children, Ellen, who is now 27, and Elizabeth, who is now 22, are both living and working in Grindon Village, Northumberland, as *'Agricultural Labourers'* with their cousin, Elizabeth Hogg.

In the 1891 Census, Margaret is still living in the Workhouse. She is now categorised as being an *'Idiot from Childhood.'* Margaret is admitted to the Northumberland County Lunatic Asylum on the 3rd June 1893, aged 63. She is listed as being *'Single'* and her *'Condition of Life and Previous Occupation'* is recorded as being *'None.'* The *'Name and Address of Relatives or Friends'* is recorded as *'Esther Tully, Duddo, Norham on Tweed.'* Her *'Place of Previous Abode'* is the *'Berwick-upon-Tweed Union Workhouse.'* Her *'Form of Mental Disease'* is recorded as *'Dementia'* and the '*Supposed Cause of Insanity*' is '*Unknown.*' The '*Duration of Existing Attacks*' is 17 years and her first attack is noted to have occurred when she was 46. Margaret dies in the County Lunatic Asylum on the 12th July, 1895, aged 65. Her cause of death is recorded as '*Acute Phthisis.*'

Margaret was a single woman with two children to support. Following the death of her parents and a period living with relatives, she enters the Workhouse. She is initially categorised as an '*Imbecile,*' but this is later changed to an '*Idiot from Childhood,*' perhaps reflecting the longstanding nature of her intellectual difficulties. Finally, she is admitted to the County Lunatic Asylum, with records indicating continued decline in her mental health. She lives there for the final two years of her life before dying of Pulmonary Tuberculosis.

Richard Whillis

Richard Whillis was born in Berwick-upon-Tweed in 1848. In the 1851 Census, aged three, he is recorded as living with his family in Church Street, Berwick-upon-Tweed. His father is Daniel S Whillis (48) and his occupation is listed as being a *'Labourer.'* His mother, Margaret Whillis, is 38. Also living at home are his siblings: Mary (19), unmarried and a *'Dressmaker,'* Jane (15), a *'Dressmaker,'* William (14), a *'Saddler's Apprentice,'* Daniel (6), a *'Scholar,'* and Isabella (one month).

In 1861, Richard is living with his family in Miller's Property, Church Street. He is now 13 and a *'Scholar.'* His siblings, living at home are: Mary (29), unmarried and a *'Dressmaker,'* Daniel (16), a *'Hairdresser,'* Isabella (10), a *'Scholar,'* and Margaret (7), a *'Scholar.'* Also, living with the family is Daniel Selby Richardson (2), who is the grandson of Richard's parents.

Ten years later, the family are still in Church Street. Richard, now 23, is listed as a *'Blacksmith out of Employment'*. His father is employed as a *'General Labourer'* and his three sisters, who are still living at home, are all *'Dressmakers.'* Richard's father dies in 1877, aged 75.

In 1881, Richard is an Inmate of the Berwick-upon-Tweed Union Workhouse. He is unmarried and his previous occupation is listed as a *'Baker.'* He is categorised as being an *'Imbecile.'* His mother and sister Mary, a *'Dressmaker,'* are living in Miller's Property, 60 Church Street.

Richard is admitted to the Northumberland County Lunatic Asylum on the 7th May 1881, aged 32. He is recorded as being unmarried and his *'Condition of Life and Previous Occupation'* is recorded as a *'Blacksmith.'* His mother, Margaret, of 58 Church Street, is listed as his family contact. His *'Place of Previous Abode'* is listed as the Workhouse. His *'Form of Mental Disease'* is recorded as *'Dementia'* and the *'Supposed Cause of Insanity'* is *'Epilepsy.'* The *'Duration of Existing Attacks'* is 15 years and the age of his first attack was at 17. Richard is discharged on the 29th August, 1881. His condition on discharge is described as *'No Improvement.'* He dies in 1883, aged 35.

Richard enters the Workhouse after the death of his father. It seems likely that he was not able to look after himself and that his family were unable to support him. He is admitted to the County Lunatic Asylum but is discharged relatively soon after. His condition appears to be epilepsy with associated cognitive decline. He dies at a relatively young age.

Jane Eleanor Wright

Jane Eleanor Wright was born in Newcastle in 1832. In the 1881 Census, aged 49, she is recorded as being an Inmate of the Berwick-upon-Tweed Union Workhouse. She is listed as being unmarried, with no previous occupation. She is categorised as being an *'Imbecile.'* In the 1891 Census, Jane is recorded as still living in the Workhouse and as being an *'Imbecile.'* She remains unmarried and is listed as having had a previous occupation as a *'Housemaid/Domestic Servant.'* Jane dies on the 9th January, 1896, in the Workhouse, aged 63. Very little further information could be found about her life and it is unclear why she was categorised as being an *'Imbecile.'*

The End of Life of the Workhouse Inmates

Many of those people, whose lives are outlined above, died in institutional care. Of those for whom place of death is known, 14 died in a Workhouse and 13 died in a Lunatic Asylum (see tables 3 and 4 overleaf).

Table 3: *'Imbeciles' in the 1881 Census who Died in Berwick-upon-Tweed Union Workhouse*

Name	Date of Death	Age at Death
Arnott, Sarah	25/7/1884	43
Bryson, Christopher	10/03/1889	78
Christie, Margaret	16/01/1883	80
Davidson, Fortune	10/12/1882	77
Dumble, John	12/11/1890	51
Fish, Jane	29/08/1882	73
Gray, Maria	02/01/1914	69
Fogon, James	26/12/1891	55
Flannigan, Ann	09/12/1891	41
Heslop, Jane	27/09/1881	46
Lovell, Patrick	25/09/1881	66
Mace, Isabella	03/10/1902	66
Wright, Jane Eleanor	09/01/1896	63

NB: Philip Spence dies in South Shields Workhouse in 1898 aged 56.

Table 4: *'Imbeciles' in the 1881 Census who Died in the Northumberland County Lunatic Asylum*

Name	Date of Death	Age at Death	Cause of Death
John Brown	31st May 1890	46	Acute Peritonitis
Matthew Campbell	21st June 1917	69	Senile Decay
Jane Dixon	9th August 1885	55	Unknown
Jane Flannigan	1924	44	Unknown
Elizabeth McNab	8th May 1898	59	Epilepsy/Congested Lung
Elizabeth Morgan	28th May 1898	48	Tuberculosis
Charles Pringle	29th March 1899	78	Tuberculosis
Bridget Robertson	29th December 1899	61	Epileptic Exhaustion
Thomas Robertson	10th October 1901	59	Cancer of the Tongue
Dorothy Scott	8th April 1914	69	Cardiovascular Disease
Elizabeth Trainer	17th February 1895	63	General Tuberculosis
Margaret Turnbull	12th July 1895	65	Acute Phthisis

NB: John Richardson died in the Huddersfield Asylum on the 9th April 1913 aged 44.

Conclusion

We have now examined the life histories of individuals categorised as *'Imbeciles'* in the 1881 Census, to the extent that these stories can be pieced together, based on the available evidence. What lessons can we draw from these stories about how people with an intellectual disability were viewed and treated during that period and how does this compare to how people are viewed today? In the final section of the book we consider these stories in the broader historical context of the lives of people categorised as having an intellectual disability.

As noted previously, many people with an intellectual disability in today's society would not be employed (Hatton, 2018) and would be unmarried (McMahon et al., 2019). The personal histories of many of those classified as *'Imbeciles,'* indicate that they had previous occupations, and some were married. A high proportion of the group also appear to have experienced mental health difficulties. The high prevalence of mental health problems in people with an intellectual disability is acknowledged today and there are an increasing number of non-drug-based interventions designed to address these difficulties (Jahoda et al., 2017). By contrast, the case notes of many of those whose lives we charted suggest few treatment approaches. Instead, there appeared to be a focus on the extent to which the person's condition allowed them to undertake some form of productive work.

A common factor for many who ended up as Inmates in the Workhouse appears to be the loss of family resources and support, following the death of the head of household or breadwinner. Those who were previously managing to cope, with family support, only become *'Idiots'* or *'Imbeciles'* when, without this support, they become paupers. The Poor Law enabled people to receive relief from poverty. An unintended consequence for those who lacked capacity, however, was that admission to the Workhouse made *'Imbeciles'* of the poor. This inadvertently condemned many to a life of institutionalisation, with little hope of returning to a normal and productive life.

From Poor Law to Medicine to Deinstitutionalisation – Lessons Learned?

The current concept, on to which the historical terms *'Idiots'* and *'Imbeciles'* map, is intellectual disability and we will use this term in this section of the book. Intellectual disability represents a certain paradox. It is, perhaps, one of the most clearly defined of all mental diagnoses, yet it is also socially determined, because the ability to function within a society depends on the extent to which that society can accommodate and support vulnerable members. The definition of intellectual disability and how it is assessed have been socially constructed throughout time and those categorised as having an intellectual disability have consistently been represented as being disenfranchised, excluded, and portrayed as a burden to society. This dates back to their representing the threat of *demonology* in the 13th century, through the burden to an educated workforce during industrialisation, the threat to societal genetic stock in the 19th century, and the threat to the health of society in the 20th century. This is an unfortunate and inaccurate characterisation of people with an intellectual disability, which overlooks the importance of affording them the appropriate support to help them flourish, despite their difficulties.

In this book, we have followed a group of people through the later phase of industrialisation and into the medicalisation of care and the associated process of *'making Imbeciles of the poor.'* The Minutes of the Board of Guardians and the Report of the Commissioners recorded therein, together with the detailed information recorded in the 1881 Census, provide an insight into the lives of people with a mild to moderate intellectual disability in the Berwick-upon-Tweed Union Workhouse at that time. The sources paint a picture of the living conditions of, and attitudes towards, people categorised as *'Imbeciles'* in the 1800s. They also suggest the ways in which government policies were interpreted and implemented at a local level, influenced by

Berwick-upon-Tweed having the unique position of being a *'County of a Town Corporate.'*

The documents also provide an opportunity to reflect on the ways in which things have changed for people with an intellectual disability since that time. While the Idiots Act was introduced in 1886, some five years after the 1881 Census, people with an intellectual disability had been categorised according to their levels of ability and functioning long before this date. The history of the concept of intellectual disability shows that the way it was understood and defined was largely determined by the dominant beliefs of what constituted a burden to society at that point and *treatment* often constituted disenfranchisement and exclusion.

Intellectual Disability as a Societal Burden

For many hundreds of years, it was believed that intellectual disability resulted from witchcraft, which required to be treated by exorcism or persecution. People who were decreed as having an intellectual disability in the 13th century were considered to be lacking in competence in the eyes of the law and their property was taken under the control of the government (Neugebauer, 1996). The individual could also be taken into custody of officials. Assessment of whether the person had an intellectual disability (referred to as an *'Idiot'* or a *'Natural Fool'* to distinguish it from mental illness) was conducted by court officials and was based on a judgement of the extent to which the person could live independently and manage the tasks required for day to day life. Assessment would relate to basic numeracy, recognition of money and if they were able to maintain a proper household (Neugebauer, 1996). These were precursors to the current criteria of cognitive and adaptive functioning. This system persisted into the mid-16th century.

Intellectual Disability as an Economic Burden

The process of industrialisation in the UK brought with it the perception of people with an intellectual disability as representing a new type of burden, this time to the need for a workforce that had the education and skills to carry out new mechanised tasks. Families moved to urban areas to work in factories, with the result that the difficulty that many people with an intellectual disability had in contributing to the workforce became more obvious (Caine et al., 1998). With the introduction of compulsory education for children, those who were deemed '*ineducable*' and, therefore, unable to contribute meaningfully to the economy, were seen as an economic burden. Categorisation was largely made on the basis of assessment of the child's literacy and numeracy skills, as well as parental reports on the child's learning (Wright, 1996). Those deemed to be '*Idiots*' were sent to separate institutions to learn the skills required to contribute to society (Gladstone, 1996). This is the period that the book has focused on, enabling us to see how the lives of 32 people, classified as having an intellectual disability, were affected by this categorisation and associated policies.

As has been seen, initially this categorisation was a way to identify people's needs in a way that would allow for the appropriate delivery of poor law relief. The resultant cost at that time, appears to have been borne by the Berwick-upon-Tweed Guild's own resources. The period that was the focus of this book represents the change from welfare support to the increasing medicalisation of many of those who were unable to support themselves.

Intellectual Disability as a Genetic Threat
The close of the 19th century saw the ascendancy of the medical profession in this area, as '*Idiocy*' became viewed as a permanent, heritable condition (Andrews, 1996; Wright, 1996) and conditions, such as Down syndrome, were identified (Digby, 1996). In addition, a more formal and standardised way for assessing intellectual disability came into being, with the setting up of the first mental testing centre by Galton around the turn of the century (Digby, 1996). The Binet-Simon Test was subsequently developed in 1905. Later tests were used in the First World War to screen recruits, as the tasks involved in

warfare become increasingly mechanised and complex. The Stanford-Binet Test was developed in 1916 and the Wechsler Tests, that are commonly used today, were developed in 1939, with regular updates from that time onwards.

It was within this context that people with an intellectual disability (now included under the term *'mental deficiency'*) were again perceived as a threat to society, along with others such as *'delinquents,' 'degenerates,'* and *'morally deficients,'* such as young unmarried mothers (Gladstone, 1996), who created societal problems (Cox, 1996). The eugenics movement proposed that those who were considered to be genetically inferior should be prevented from breeding. As such, people with an intellectual disability, at that time considered to be a heritable condition, would be segregated from the general population and prevented from having children (Caine et al. 1998; Digby, 1998). The result, segregated institutional care, was seen as a means of protecting society from people with an intellectual disability (Jackson, 1996).

Intellectual Disability as an Illness

The original Poor Laws were a largely social endeavour, with the aim of protecting the health and wellbeing of the population, so that an adequate workforce could be maintained. Administering such a system was often left to local officials and the church. Medical roles were not properly developed until the 1800s, with the first clear role being established by the General Medical Order in 1842. Initially the role of doctors was largely administrative, deciding how welfare should be granted and looking after the general health of poor people at times of need. At this time, there were very few medical treatments available and the *prescriptions* were often for beef, wine, and flour for adults and milk for children. A further role for doctors was to decide whether people fell into the categories of the *deserving* or *undeserving* poor, as this would determine how a person would be treated. Allowances were made for people who suffered through no fault of their own and who lacked the capacity to provide for their own means. Others, deemed to be capable, would be expected to work their way back to financial independence.

Defining people by their capacity was not a new idea in the provision of poor relief, but it was to take a new direction with the increased role of the medical profession. The role of categorisation was to become expanded as the early days of diagnosing people's problems began to be established more formally. People were already treated differently if they were *deserving* or *undeserving*, but clearer distinctions began to be made between the categories of people who were either '*Lunatics*' or '*Idiots*.' The Lunacy Act of 1845 led to the further growth of County Lunatic Asylums and '*Lunacy*' became subdivided into various subtypes, for example, '*mania*' (an elevated mood), '*melancholia*' (a depressed mood), '*dementia*' (mental decline), '*monomania*' (insanity relating to a single issue in the context of an otherwise sane person), and '*delusional insanity*' (thoughts and beliefs that are not based in reality). Epilepsy was still considered a '*form of insanity*' in the 1800s and it interesting to note that its care moved from Psychiatry to Neurology as more successful forms of treatment were discovered in the twentieth century.

The Idiots Act of 1886 produced a similar growth in County institutions specialising in training and education, but initially those who could not be catered for in Workhouses were placed in County Lunatic Asylums. Clearer distinctions were made between '*Imbeciles*' and '*Idiots*,' with '*Idiocy*' being defined as a more severe disability present from childhood, while '*Imbecility*' was a more moderate form of mental incapacity, that could also be acquired later in life as a result of, for example, illness, injury, or dementia.

As institutional care became available as an alternative to wards in Workhouses, so the role of doctors and the medical model expanded, reflected, not only in the way services were delivered, but also in the way people were treated. County Lunatic Asylums became County Mental Hospitals and paupers became patients. In Northumberland, the advent of large institutions, such as Northgate Hospital, Morpeth, which was established in 1914 and, initially called St Andrew's Colony, heralded the beginning of the centralisation of resources and the distancing of people with intellectual disabilities from their families and communities.

Medicalisation led to an increased expectancy of treatment, the introduction of case notes, and the idea that people's conditions should be improving. Regular medical reviews took place, but unfortunately, as we have seen, the notes often recorded a lack of progress or *'no change'* as people often had intractable problems. There is a dearth of information about the lives of people, beyond their physical health, their categorisation, and their ability to work. We learn little about them as people. We discover nothing about their interests, aspirations, or preferences. We don't find out anything about their social relationships with families, friends, and other people, or the many factors that influence wider quality of life.

In the 1800s, medical treatment was very limited and quite basic. People categorised as *'Imbeciles'* and *'Idiots'* were, by definition, not able to be cured and often languished under this system of care. Case notes became increasingly negative and the language used to categorise and describe people became harsher and dismissive. As the number of people institutionalised rapidly grew in the second half of the 1800s, *'Imbecility'* and *'Idiocy'* were viewed less as reasons to consider people as being *deserving* of care and more as reasons for being incurable and burdensome. This resulted in a heightened process of *othering*.

The Othering of People with an Intellectual Disability
Othering is the process of treating people, or groups of people, as being intrinsically different or alien to yourself. Psychiatrists were once called Alienists, perhaps reflecting their role in identifying and categorising people who were considered to differ significantly from accepted norms. The process of othering can be seen to evolve over time, as exemplified by the attempts by the Berwick-upon-Tweed Union to provide for poor, ill and disabled people.

The early Poor Laws were based on some simple principles. People were viewed as having an inherent value and poor relief was designed to provide some protection at times of need. In the early 1800s, there appears to have been less need to categorise people as being *'Imbeciles'* and *'Idiots,'* due to the existence of a greater number of roles that allowed them to contribute economically, rather than being perceived as a burden. In particular, the economy of Berwick-upon-Tweed was largely agrarian and non-mechanised and, therefore, reliant on a seasonal workforce, especially at harvest time. In this context, the Poor Law offered a means of looking after this valuable workforce in times of hardship, to ensure they would be available when needed.

The combined effects of the end of the Napoleonic Wars and the Industrial Revolution, meant that there were fewer roles for people who were less able and there was an increasing demand on poor relief as the numbers of people requiring assistance grew. As the demand for labour reduced, those who were unable to work were devalued and there was an increase in the use of categorisation, exacerbating the effects of othering.

This process accelerates further with the introduction of the medical model, which fundamentally categorises and defines people by what is *wrong* with them. Increased institutionalisation worsens this process, as those who are institutionalised become isolated from their families, communities, and local economies, and any valued roles that they had previously held there. Ultimately, these people become defined by what they cost to their Parishes. The Parishes, however, have less influence over how costs are incurred and limited control over the processes that determine whether people return to their communities and economies or not.

The othering process is illustrated by the entries in the case-notes of those who were institutionalised. They are often referred to in inhuman ways and their names are rarely used, with people being referred to by their categorisations, such as, *'this idiot,' 'patient,' 'this epileptic,'* or simply as *'P.'* The narrative itself also becomes increasingly distant and negative. For example, Jane Flannigan's notes state: *'This imbecile remains as childish and stupid as ever,*' John Richardson is described as being '*Still as much like a monkey as ever,*' Thomas Robertson is '*Very stupid. Simply says "Aye and No,"*"' while Elizabeth McNab is '*Quite stupid,*' and Matthew Campbell is a '*little stunted idiot…without intelligence. He cannot speak.*'

The case notes, while designed to record medical progress, have little relevance to those who were followed up in our study. As they fail to improve under the regime, their notes get shorter, less detailed, and often simply state '*no change.*' There seems no clear medical reason for why some people are discharged and some remain in institutions, with some people remaining in the County Lunatic Asylum for some considerable time after being assessed as fit for discharge, while others are discharged despite '*no improvement*' in their condition. They are ultimately defined and categorised by their limited functioning and lack of ability to improve their condition. As a result, people are often unable to move on from institutional care. The numbers in institutions continue to grow as the approach to the problem of impoverished people becomes the problem itself. Increased numbers of people become a greater burden and cost to the economy, with a resulting growth in categorisation and negative narratives about vulnerable people.

Deinstitutionalisation
The medical model of care predominated for many years and the threat that people with an intellectual disability posed remained one of representing sub-optimal health, failure to improve, and lack of economic value. This model began to be challenged in the 1960s. The advent of the civil rights movement and the philosophy of normalisation (Wolfensberger, 1972), along with a number of institutional scandals, which highlighted the abuse of people with an intellectual disability (Race, 1995), contributed to a shift in the view of people with intellectual disability as a burden to society. It was advocated that this group of people should be afforded the same opportunities and rights as the rest of society (Caine et al., 1998). This shift in the political agenda

resulted in the introduction of the Community Care Act in 1990 and the beginning of hospital closures. Community Learning Disability Teams began to emerge throughout the 1980s and, although providing services to those living at home, they became actively involved in service development and the deinstitutionalisation process (Brown & Wistow, 1990).

From the 1980s onwards, a number of UK government polices emerged which, although not directly targeted at people with an intellectual disability, nevertheless impacted upon their lives in areas such as education, housing, health, and social inclusion. In 2000 (Scottish Executive, 2000) and 2001 (Department of Health, 2001), national government policy was developed specifically with the aims of addressing the needs of people with an intellectual disability, ensuring their voices were heard in issues relating to them, and that they were included as part of local communities and society as a whole. In 2014, following further abuse scandals, ending the inappropriate care of people with an intellectual disability in institutions became a government priority (NHS England, 2014).

Current Conceptualisation of People with an Intellectual Disability
Despite these changes and attempts to move from deficit models of disability towards defining people with an intellectual disability as individuals with a valued identity and role in society, the predominant way of thinking remains largely based on the medical model. This primarily views people with an intellectual disability as having something *wrong* with them. While it is necessary to have a method of identifying those who require additional help because of disability, the diagnostic criteria for intellectual disability still define people in terms of significant deficits (APA, 2013). In addition, the term intellectual disability continues to be associated with a stigmatised identity (Paterson et al., 2012).

There is also evidence that people with an intellectual disability continue to be seen as constituting a moral threat to society. This is exemplified in two main ways: the continued segregation of many people with an intellectual disability in institutional care and the over-representation of people with an intellectual disability in criminal justice services. Institutionalisation today is often rationalised as a means of supporting those who display *'behaviours that challenge.'* This is despite a lack of evidence that in-patient provision is more effective than community-based services (McKenzie, 2011). As was also evidenced with many of the people in this book, once in an institutional setting, people with an intellectual disability in modern times are at risk of remaining, even when their treatment is complete (McKenzie, 2011).

Evidence suggests that people with an intellectual disability are over-represented within criminal justice services, including prison (Jones, 2007; Søndenaa et al., 2008). Rather than evidencing that people with an intellectual disability are more likely to commit crimes i.e. are a genuine moral threat to society, many may end up in prison, because their intellectual disability is not recognised (McKenzie et al., 2012) and they may, therefore, not understand the criminal proceedings or be given appropriate support to navigate them.

There are indications that people with an intellectual disability also continue to be perceived as a genetic threat. This is demonstrated in the attitudes towards, and control of, behaviour that relates to relationships, sexual expression, and parenthood. The sexuality of many people with an intellectual disability is constrained and controlled (Sullivan et al., 2014), they are significantly more likely to be single than their typically developing peers, (McMahon et al., 2019), and parents with an intellectual disability are likely to be viewed negatively, with an assumption of parental incompetence (see McKenzie et al., 2015 for an overview). This denies people with an intellectual disability the positive identity of an adult who has contributed to society through the mechanism of the family.

The perception of people with an intellectual disability as an economic burden is also present in today's society, with employment rates of working age people with an intellectual disability being significantly lower than for those without, at 5.7% in England. In addition, fewer women with an intellectual disability are employed compared with men (Hatton, 2018). This contrasts with the people in the Workhouse categorised as *'Imbeciles'* in 1881, of whom 53% had been in prior employment. Thus, the figures suggest that the majority of people with an intellectual disability today are denied the opportunity to be a financial asset, rather than being perceived as an economic burden.

Conclusion

In this book we have charted the process, whereby people who were largely coping and often contributing members of their communities, albeit frequently with the support of family or partners, became Inmates of the Workhouse when these systems of support and work roles were no longer in place. The resultant poverty led to the first categorisation of this group as *'poor,'* with the subsequent determination of whether they are *deserving* or *undeserving* resulting in the further classification of them as *'Idiots'* or *'Imbeciles.'* For many of this group, their categorisation and institutionalisation in Workhouses and Asylums, under what becomes a medical model of care, results in a process of *othering*, whereby they are viewed negatively and as an economic, and subsequently moral, threat to society.

Despite current positive philosophical and political stances, people with an intellectual disability continue to be diagnosed by criteria that define them as *outliers* and categorised by what they are *not capable* of. The root of the problem – depriving people of the opportunity to engage in things they can do and experience valued roles – is still not being adequately addressed. If people are in a position to contribute to society, they are by definition, an asset. If not, they are at risk of being perceived as a cost and a burden and of being categorised negatively, with the associated economics of increasing care and, ultimately, medical intervention. Put simply, if we know what is *right* about people and what they *can* do, they can take part and do their bit. If we continue to focus on the limitations of people with an intellectual disability, they will continue to be represented as a burden to society. This is currently managed by controlling and largely excluding this group from the roles and rituals associated with key valued life transitions: relationships, sex, parenthood, and work.

On the positive side, many people with an intellectual disability today do not experience segregated and impoverished lives. The majority live with their families or in their own homes, with support. Government policies, such as Transforming Care (NHS England, 2014) have resulted in a further reduction in inappropriate institutional care; screening tools exist to help identify people with an intellectual disability at an early stage in the criminal justice system, in order for them to receive appropriate support (McKenzie et al., 2012), and there is a growing acceptance and use of positive behavioural approaches to improve the quality of life and manage the behaviours that challenge that are displayed by those whose needs are not being met appropriately (PBS Coalition UK, 2015). In addition, while people with an intellectual disability continue to experience significant health inequalities (Emerson et al., 2012), advances in psychotherapeutic approaches (Jahoda et al., 2017) and the introduction of reasonable adjustments in health care provision (NHS England, 2018) have been instrumental in improving the health and wellbeing of many.

Afterword

In writing this book, we hope that we have appropriately honoured the lives of those people who appear to have had limited experience of being valued during their lifetime. Looking back, there are many lessons we can learn from the way things were done in the past. While we cannot ignore the substantial improvements in people's health and living conditions since the 1800s, it would be remiss to not also address areas where mistakes continue to be made. The original Poor Laws were relatively uncomplicated. The majority of people lived in rural areas and, even people with limited abilities were able to find some kind of work to sustain themselves. People were valued because they were needed to work on the land, and they were looked after in times of need. People who had wealth were expected to contribute to poor relief as, even though work might be seasonal, people were needed to bring in the harvest, so keeping them alive through the winter was important.

Workhouses were often set up with the best intentions and even County Lunatic Asylums were originally set up as places of safety, where people could be kept healthy and trained to work, with the expressed intention of returning people to valued roles in society. Unfortunately, the way in which institutions evolved led them to become a part of the medicalising and othering of undervalued people, often condemning them to a life excluded from their communities and families.

Today, we continue to repeat these errors. Categorising people in a way that identifies what is *wrong* with them might work well in areas of physical medicine, where there are conditions for which there are treatments, remedies, and cures, but it does not provide the answers when people's difficulties are socially constructed. In such circumstances, the way forward is always to also understand what is *right* about people. Solutions come from understanding how people function and by making sure there are roles in society for everyone to contribute in a way that is valued. History tells us that it is certainly more costly for society as a whole not to do so.

Finally, we need to be clear about where the '*Idiocy*,' '*Imbecility*,' and '*Lunacy*' lie in society. Are they features of the people categorised in such a manner, or are they embodied in the policies and processes that create them?

References: Main Sources

Board of Guardians of Berwick-upon-Tweed Poor Law Union Minute Book.

Cowe, J.D. (2018). *The Development of Education in Berwick-upon-Tweed to 1902*. Edited and Published by Jonathan Cowe.

Fuller, J. (1799). *The History of Berwick-upon-Tweed: Including a Short Account of the Villages of Tweedmouth and Spittal*. Ulan Press.

Johnston, T. (1817). *The History of Berwick-upon-Tweed and its Vicinity*.

Northumberland County Archives – Record Books of St George's Hospital, Morpeth.

Sheldon, F. (1849). *History of Berwick-upon-Tweed*. Historical Collection from the British Library.

Scott, J. (1888). *The History of Berwick-upon-Tweed. The History of the Town and Guild*. Historical Collection from the British Library.

UK Census Records 1841. 1851, 1861, 1871, 1881, 1891, 1901, 1911.

Rawlinson, R. (1850). *Report to the General Board of Health on a Preliminary Inquiry into the Sewerage, Drainage, and Supply of Water, and the Sanitation Condition of the Inhabitants, of the Parish of Berwick-upon-Tweed, in the County of the Borough and Town of the same, including the Townships of Tweedmouth and Spittal*.

Additional References

American Psychiatric Association. (2013). *Diagnostic and Statistical Manual of Mental Disorders.* 5th Edition. Washington, DC: American Psychiatric Association.

Andrews, J. (1996). Identifying and providing for the mentally disabled in early modern London. In D. Wright & A. Digby (Eds.), *From Idiocy to Mental Deficiency: Historical perspectives on people with learning disabilities.* London: Routledge.

Beadle-Brown, J., Mansell, J. L., Whelton, B., Hutchinson, A., & Skidmore, C. (2006). People with learning disabilities in 'out-of-area' residential placements: 2. Reasons for and effects of placement. *Journal of Intellectual Disability Research, 50* (11), 845-856.

Borthwick-Duffy, S. (1994). Prevalence of destructive behaviours. In T. Thompson & D. B. Gray (Eds) *Destructive Behaviour in Developmental Disabilities: Diagnosis and Treatment.* London: Sage.

British Psychological Society (2001). *Learning Disability: Definitions and contexts.* British Psychological Society, Leicester.

Brown, S. & Wistow, G. (1990). *The Roles and Tasks of CMHT'S.* Aldershot: Avebury.

Caine, A., Hatton, C., & Emerson, E. (1998). Service Provision. In E. Emerson, C. Hatton, J. Bromley, & A. Caine. *Clinical Psychology and people with Intellectual Disabilities.* Chichester: Wiley.

Cox, P. (1996). Girls, deficiency and delinquency. In D. Wright & A. Digby (Eds.), *From Idiocy to Mental Deficiency: Historical perspectives on people with learning disabilities.* London: Routledge.

Department of Health. (1991). *NHS Community Care Act.* London. HMSO.

Department of Health. (2001). *Valuing People: A New Strategy for Learning Disability for the 21st Century.* UK: Ibid.

Digby, A. (1996). Contexts and Perspectives. In D. Wright & A. Digby (Eds.), *From Idiocy to Mental Deficiency: Historical perspectives on people with learning disabilities.* London: Routledge.

Emerson, E., Baines, S., Allerton, L., & Welch, V. (2012). *Health inequalities and people with learning disabilities in the UK.* Durham, UK: Improving Health & Lives: Learning Disabilities Observatory.

Gladstone, D. (1996). The changing dynamic of institutional care: The Western Counties Idiot Asylum, 1864-1914. In D. Wright & A. Digby (Eds.), *From Idiocy to Mental Deficiency: Historical perspectives on people with learning disabilities.* London: Routledge.

Hatton, C. (2018). Paid employment amongst adults with learning disabilities receiving social care in England: trends over time and geographical variation. *Tizard Learning Disability Review, 23*(2), 117-122.

Healthcare Commission and Commission for Social Care Inspection (2006). *Joint Investigation into the Provision of Services for People with Learning Disabilities at Cornwall Partnership NHS Trust.* London: Healthcare Commission.

Jackson, M. (1996). Institutional provision for the feeble-minded in Edwardian England: Sandlebridge and the scientific morality of permanent care. In D. Wright & A. Digby (Eds.), *From Idiocy to Mental Deficiency: Historical perspectives on people with learning disabilities.* London: Routledge.

Jahoda, A., Stenfert-Kroese, B., & Pert, C. (2017). *Cognitive Behaviour Therapy for People with Intellectual Disabilities.* London: Palgrave MacMillan.

Jones, J. (2007). Persons with intellectual disabilities in the criminal justice system: review of issues. *International Journal of Offender Therapy and Comparative Criminology, 51*(6), 723-733.

McMahon, M., Bowring, D.L., & Hatton, C. (2019). Not such an ordinary life: a comparison of employment, marital status and housing profiles of adults with and without intellectual disabilities. *Tizard Learning Disability Review, 24* (4), 213-221.

McKenzie, K. (2011). Providing services in the United Kingdom to people with an intellectual disability who present behaviour which challenges: A review of the literature. *Research in Developmental Disabilities, 32,* 395–403,

McKenzie, K., Michie, A., Murray, A.L., & Hales, C. (2012). Screening for offenders with an intellectual disability: the validity of the Learning Disability Screening Questionnaire. *Research in Developmental Disabilities, 33,* 791-795

McKenzie, K., Wilson, S., & Shewan, L. (2015). Rights of individuals with disability to parenthood. in Rubin, I.L., Merrick, J., Greydanus, D.E. & Patel, D.R. (Eds.) *Health Care for people with Intellectual and Developmental Disabilities across the lifespan.* Switzerland: Springer.

Moore, A.M. & O'Brien, K. (2006). Follow-up issues with multiples. *Paediatrics Child Health, 11*(5), 283-286.

Neugebauer, R. (1996). Mental handicap in medieval and early modern England: Criteria, measurement and care. In D. Wright & A. Digby (Eds.), *From Idiocy to Mental Deficiency: Historical perspectives on people with learning disabilities.* London: Routledge.

NHS England (2014). Winterbourne View – Time for Change: Transforming the commissioning of services for people with learning disabilities and/or autism. [Available at: www.england.nhs.uk/wp-content/uploads/2014/11/transforming-commissioning-services.pdf]

NHS England (2018). *The Government response to the learning disabilities mortality review (LeDeR) programme second annual report.* Leeds, UK: Department of Health and Social Care.

Paterson, L., McKenzie, K., & Lindsay, W.R. (2011). Stigma, Social Comparison and Self-Esteem in adults with an Intellectual Disability. *Journal of Applied Research in Intellectual Disabilities. 25*(2), 166–176.

Positive Behavioural Support (PBS) Coalition UK (2015). *Positive Behavioural Support: A Competence Framework.* Ibid. Available at: www.pbsacademy.org.uk/wp-content/uploads/2016/11/Positive-Behavioural-Support-Competence-Framework-May-2015.pdf

Race, D. (1994). Historical development of service provision. In N. Malin. *Services for people with learning disabilities* (Eds). London: Routledge.

Romeo, R., Knapp, M., Tyer, P., Crawford, M., & Oliver-Africano, P. (2009). The treatment of challenging behaviour in intellectual disabilities: cost-effectiveness analysis. *Journal of Intellectual Disability Research*, 53(7), 633-634.

Scottish Executive. (2000). *The same as you? A review of services for people with learning disabilities.* Edinburgh: Scottish Executive.

Scottish Executive. (2000). *Adults with Incapacity (Scotland) Act.* London: The Stationery Office.

Scottish Office. (1998). *Interviewing people who are mentally disordered: Appropriate Adult Schemes.* Edinburgh: Scottish Office.

Søndenaa, E., Palmstierna, T., & Iversen, V. C. (2010). A step-wise approach to identifying intellectual disabilities in the criminal justice system. *European Journal of Psychology Applied to Legal Context*, 2(2), 183–198.

Søndenaa, E., Rasmussen, K., Palmstierna, T., & Nottestad, J.A. (2008). The prevalence and nature of intellectual disability in Norwegian prisons. *Journal of Intellectual Disability Research*, 52, 1129-1137.

Sturmey, P. (2009). Restraint, seclusion and PRN medication in English services for people with learning disabilities administered by the National Health Service: An analysis of the 2007 National Audit Survey. *Journal of Applied Research in Intellectual Disabilities*, 22, 140-144.

Sullivan F, Bowden K, McKenzie K, & Quayle E. (2013). 'Touching people in relationships': A qualitative study of close relationships for people with an intellectual disability. *Journal of Clinical Nursing*, 22, 3456-66.

Wright, D. (1996). 'Childlike in his innocence': Lay attitudes to 'idiots' and 'imbeciles' in Victorian England. In D. Wright & A. Digby (Eds.), *From Idiocy to Mental Deficiency: Historical perspectives on people with learning disabilities*. London: Routledge.

Wolfensberger, W. (1972). *The principle of normalisation in human services.* Toronto: National Institute of Mental Retardation.

Appendix: Berwick-upon-Tweed Union Workhouse Timeline

1388	The Poor Law Act (Attempts to address labour shortages following Black death).
1494	The Vagabonds and Beggars Act (Introduces punishment as a strategy).
1531	The Revised Vagabonds and Beggars Act (Allows licences to be given to the infirm, elderly and disabled to beg).
1536-1541	The Dissolution of the Monasteries (Leads to transfer of resources from the church to the crown).
1552	The Poor Law Act (Focuses on using Parish resources to combat poverty).
1576	Act establishing Houses of Correction.
1578	Transfer of power to administer the Poor Law from Justices to Church Officials.
1601	The Poor Law Act establishing Parishes as being responsible for their communities.
1657	Establishment of a House of Correction in Berwick-upon-Tweed.
1662	The Poor Relief Act (The Settlement Act).
1681	The Berwick-upon-Tweed House of Correction is demolished.
1723	The Workhouse Test.
1752	The Vagabonds Act.
1758	The Berwick-upon-Tweed Workhouse opens in Church Street.
1803	Establishment of New Workhouse in former Berwick-upon-Tweed sack manufactory.
1813	Establishment of the Royal Edinburgh Asylum.
1813	New Lunatic Asylum and Schoolhouse added to the Berwick-upon-Tweed Workhouse site.
1815	End of the Napoleonic Wars.
1824	The Vagrancy Act leads to homeless people being housed overnight in Workhouse.
1834	The New Poor Law Act (Emphasises the use of Workhouses).
1835	The Municipal Reform Act.
1836	Establishment of Berwick-upon-Tweed Union.
1842	The General Medical Order.
1845	The Lunacy Act.
1846	Irremovable Poor Act
1859	Establishment of the Northumberland County Pauper Lunatic Asylum.
1886	The Idiots Act.
1913	The Mental Deficiency Act.
1914	Establishment of St Andrew's Colony for the Mentally Defective, Northgate, Morpeth.
1930	Abolition of the Workhouse system.